GHOSTS' WHO'S WHO

Ghosts' Who's Who

JACK HALLAM

DAVID & CHARLES
NEWTON ABBOT   LONDON   NORTH POMFRET (VT)   VANCOUVER

To Alison Elizabeth

ISBN 0 7153 7452 4
Library of Congress Catalog Card Number 77-89382

© Jack Hallam 1977

All rights reserved. No part of this publication may be reproduced, stored in a retrieval system, or transmitted, in any form or by any means, electronic, mechanical, photocopying, recording or otherwise, without the prior permission of David & Charles (Publishers) Limited

Set in 11 on 13pt Garamond
and printed in Great Britain by Latimer Trend & Company Ltd Plymouth
for David & Charles (Publishers) Limited
Brunel House Newton Abbot Devon

Published in the United States of America
by David & Charles Inc
North Pomfret Vermont 05053 USA

Published in Canada
by Douglas David & Charles Limited
1875 Welch Street North Vancouver BC

FOREWORD

Grey ladies are ten-a-penny. So too are the hooded figures of monks, black canons, white friars and other variously tinted phantoms. Along with high-booted cavaliers, baying hounds, and lurching coaches pulled by headless horses, they dominate the written evidence on ghosts and hauntings.

This *Who's Who* is not so much about those ghosts as about the members of the phantom community that have an identity; the ghosts to which a name has been put, be they royals or rogues, Bronze-Age or jet-set, princes or paupers.

From the outset, the limitations of a book of this size precluded all the Scottish and Irish spectral population, for which I am truly sorry, since Celtic ghosts are such a bonny lot. I also apologise if, in my selection, I have omitted your favourite ghost, or left out a positively identified, long-established phantom with a pedigree going back to the cavemen of the Mendips. Because, when selecting the material, I paid more attention to the 'who' and 'why' of a haunting, and less to atmosphere and spine-chilling details of the actual ghostly encounters, I have compiled a very comprehensive bibliography. Every one of the books listed is recommended as first-class reading, whether you believe in ghosts or not. I could not have compiled this *Who's Who* without recourse to those books, and to the stories published in magazines and newspapers almost every day.

I am sincerely grateful to all the authors and journalists to whose work I referred, and to all those other people who kindly supplied me with information, by letter or word of mouth, particularly Mrs Peggy Jackson, Mr Kenneth Bird, Mr Alfred Mills and Mr Charles Selway. Finally, I am immensely indebted to my daughter Angela, and June, my wife, for the typing and scrutiny of this manuscript as well as for their understanding and patience.

Jack Hallam
February 1977　　　　　　　　　　　　　　　Reigate, Surrey

The district after each title name is the latest known haunt of the ghost referred to, and the map and key at the end of the book indicate the approximate locations of each.

Jeremiah Abershaw—Wimbledon, London

Jeremiah Abershaw was one who had some rich pickings from highway robbery. The 1,000 acre Wimbledon Common was largely his territory, though, for the sake of a fat purse or a jewel-covered bosom, he ranged across Putney Heath to the much-travelled Portsmouth Road. He ventured his luck once too often, however, got caught redhanded, and went to the gallows on Wimbledon Hill in 1795. He left behind a reputation for daring and ruthlessness—and a ghost which has been reported on the common and heath astride a galloping steed.

Lady Abigail—Featherstone Castle, Northumberland

Abigail was Baron Featherstonehaugh's only daughter, ghostly leading-lady in the profusion of phantoms haunting this castle and as far as the Roman Wall, three miles to the north. Against her will, Abigail married a distant relative called Timothy Featherstonehaugh who rode with her at the head of the celebration hunt which followed their wedding. In the woods at Pynkin Cleugh, they ran headlong into an ambush led by young Ridley of Hardriding, the bride's thwarted suitor, and, in the ensuing battle, Abigail died trying to stop her husband fighting to the death with the man she loved. Since that tragic day, many have reported seeing the spectral hunt galloping towards the woods at dusk. Others have talked of a ghostly sight, even more terrifying, as the entire bridal party, led by the Lady Abigail, returns silently to the castle, their faces ashen masks of death, their eyes glazed and staring.

Elizabeth Adams—Swanbourne, Buckinghamshire

Thomas Adams, murdered by 'bloudy theves' in October 1627, left behind four children and a young widow named Elizabeth.

All the family is depicted on a wellworn memorial brass in the village church of St Swithin's. By that, the people of the village recognise that the Green Lady, who has haunted this part of Buckinghamshire for 300 years, is the restless ghost of the broken-hearted Elizabeth, searching for those who destroyed her happiness.

Father Ambrose—Wardley Hall, Worsley, Greater Manchester

In a recess at the top of a staircase in Wardley are the remains of a skull, all that is left of the head of Father Ambrose (born Edward Barlow, of Old Barlow Hall), hanged at Lancaster in 1641 for the crime of spreading the forbidden Catholic religion. Tradition has it that to remove the gruesome relic from the Hall has dire results, like the time a new maid threw it into the moat and 'a terrible tempest' rocked the house. Only when the moat was dragged and the skull returned, did the storm abate. Disturbances followed whenever the skull was removed, resulting in a clause in the lease forbidding its removal.

Bishop Lancelot Andrews—Cheam, Surrey

Bishop Lancelot packed a great deal of living into his sixty-one years. He was a firm favourite of Queen Elizabeth, was well thought of at the Court of James I, and, in turn, was Bishop of Chichester, Ely and Winchester. Yet, it was the quiet life at the red brick rectory in Cheam he seemingly enjoyed the most, since that is where his ghost is said to haunt, visible only from the knees upwards, due to a change in floor levels at some time in the house's history.

In the more modern centre of Cheam, the old Century Cinema, lately converted to a motor-car salesroom, boasts the ghost of a carpenter who disappeared without trace, while the cinema was being built in the 1930s.

Queen Anne's Messenger—Carshalton House, Sutton, London

Dr John Radcliffe, physician to Queen Anne, bought Carshalton House in 1713, without considering his commuting problems. It was too far out of town to answer a royal summons in a hurry and when Queen Anne, crippled with gout, sent word calling him urgently to her bedside, he flatly refused. The Queen's messenger remonstrated with Dr John, who flew into a rage and flung the man down the main staircase, breaking his neck, a death which gave the house the first of its many ghosts. The doctor never had to face trial, since he went into a decline and died soon afterwards. The next owner, Sir John Fellowes, after a violent row with the tax collector, pushed that unfortunate fellow over the balustrade. Some say his ghost also haunts the same stairway.

Lord John Angerstein—Greenwich, London

John Julius Angerstein amassed a fabulous fortune in his lifetime, with which he bought property and pictures. Forty of the exquisite masterpieces, which once adorned the walls of his East Greenwich home on Vanburgh Hill, were bought by the nation for £57,000, in 1824, to form the nucleus of the National Gallery. Lord John did not live to see that day; he died the year before, leaving a ghost as opulent as he was in his lifetime. It is said his phantom coach still drives out on winter nights to the Ship and Billet Inn to collect his lordship, resplendent in black velvet, silk hose and silver buckled shoes.

Annie—Wandsworth Prison, London

She is the dejected figure of a woman of middle-age, dressed in old-style prison grey, seen moving silently along the vaulted corridors of this Victorian 'house of correction'. To prisoners and prison officers she is known as Wandsworth Annie, believed to be the spectre of a prisoner who died while doing time some twenty years after the jail was opened, in 1851, with accommodation for more than a thousand criminals of both sexes.

Fred Archer—Newmarket, Suffolk

Archer was a top jockey of the Victorian turf. Before he died in 1886, age twenty-nine, he'd ridden at least 2,000 winners, twenty of them in classics. Although the Epsom Derby was one of his favourite rides—he won it five times—Newmarket is where he haunts, out on the heath, and in Hamilton Stud Lane, mounted on the grey horse of which he was most fond. His ghost is thought to have caused some of the unexplained racing mishaps on the Newmarket course.

Anne Armstrong—Wellington Hotel, Riding Mill, Northumberland

Anne Armstrong was a servant-girl turned witch-hunter, on whose evidence five witches of Northumberland were tried at Morpeth in the summer of 1673. Those who talked their way out of being burnt alive on a pile of faggots, took revenge on Anne after luring her to a small back kitchen of what is now the Wellington. With a rope that was supposed to have magical powers, they hanged her, since when her ghost has periodically revisited the place of execution.

Archie Armstrong—Haughton Castle, Northumberland

It was in the reign of Henry VIII that the notorious Archie Armstrong met his agonising end at Haughton, and over the ensuing centuries his outraged ghost has many times returned to the castle dungeon in which he accidentally died of slow starvation. Armstrong, leader of a gang of reivers caught in Sir John Widdrington's Haughton estate, stealing cattle, was bundled into a cell while Sir John rode to York to confer urgently with Cardinal Wolsey. Not until Sir John reached York did he realise he had shut up his prisoner without food or water and pocketed the key.

Squire John Arscott—Tetcott, Devon

Squire John, the last of the Arscotts, haunts the Devon countryside around the old family home at Tetcott. He was an eighteenth-century eccentric who went to church on Sunday to throw apples at the vicar and feed the church spiders on flies which he carried in a bottle. His favourite horse was Blackbird, a phantom form of which his ghost is seen riding, with the pack in full cry.

King Athelstan—Dacre Castle, Cumbria

If legend is to be believed this royal ghost has been haunting here for a thousand years, in the company of two other kings of his day —Constantine of Scotland and Owain of Cumbria. They met here in AD 926 to discuss their differences peacefully, but succeeded only in engaging in bigger and bloodier battles, culminating in a Saxon massacre at Brunanburgh.

Jack Arthur—Spring Lane, Shotley Bridge, County Durham

Postal workers, making early morning deliveries in Spring Lane, have encountered the ghost of Jack Arthur, a twenty-two-year-old paper-mill worker who disappeared from his lodgings in nearby Snow's Green Road, in 1895. From that year on—until his ghost was first seen in December 1970—Jack Arthur was not heard of again after starting to walk to work at 7.30 one winter's morning. His disappearance followed a midnight quarrel with his landlord, postman Jack Rutherford, who objected to his lodger drinking and gambling.

King Arthur—Cadbury Castle, Somerset

The real Arthur was a British chieftain who lived around AD 500 and fought with great distinction against the Saxons. The legendary Arthur, surrounded by swashbuckling knights and lovely ladies, is not so easy to pigeonhole. Tradition has his ghost haunting in almost all the places in which the legendary King set foot, though South Cadbury comes nearest, archaeologically, to having any real rating as the site of Camelot and is the most likely to be ghosted by him. A phantom Arthur is reputed to ride, on mid-summer's eve, at the head of a string of spectral knights, across a causeway a mile or two north of Cadbury Castle where, on winter's nights, the sounds of baying hounds and shouting men are heard as Arthur takes his warriors hunting. While ruined Tintagel Castle, Arthur's supposed Cornish birthplace, claims an Arthurian spectre, Glastonbury is thought to be the Isle of Avalon where the King lies buried beside Queen Guinevere, but it is only she who lingers here, as a radiant female phantom. Motorists on the road which skirts the Gower Peninsula, have seen an armoured spectre which, it is suggested, may be Arthur. He materialises from a hillside barrow and then disappears on the seashore at Llanrhidian, Glamorgan.

Lady Blanche Arundell—Old Wardour, Wiltshire

Lady Blanche, with only twenty-five trained men, withstood the Roundhead seige of old Wardour Castle for five long days in May 1643. Had it not been for the ladies-in-waiting and their maids constantly reloading muskets and supplying the men with food, the Parliamentary Army, 1,300 strong, could never have been kept so long at bay. Many of the women were injured, some killed, and the ghost of one still haunts this crumbling pile. Some say it is Lady Blanche herself, walking at dusk towards the lake opposite the castle.

Lady St Aubyn—Richmond, Surrey

In her autobiography *What Shall We Do Tomorrow*, Mary Hayley Bell, playwright and wife of actor John Mills, says this of Lady St Aubyn, the ghost of The Wick on Richmond Hill:

> She walks up the stairs from the dining room dressed in a grey Inverness cloak. She built the house in 1775 on the foundations of what was once the Bull Inn. Robert Myline was the architect and Daniel Pinder the builder ... Lady St Aubyn was a great hostess. She loved the arts and all sorts of people came here—George III, of course, and Sir Joshua Reynolds, who lived next door and painted from the balcony ...

B

The Ballet Dancer—Dulwich, London

On warm summer evenings the quiet glades of One Tree Hill are well populated with young lovers, most of whom are aware that this wooded corner of Honor Oak Park adjoins a cemetery. Not so many know of the ghostly presence of a dancing girl who shares their seclusion. She is about twenty, with long, fair hair, wears an open black coat, a small white apron and performs happily with movements that are balletic, light and noiseless. Author Andrew MacKenzie first revealed this phantom dancer, who remains unidentified, in his book *Frontiers of the Unknown*.

Old Barbery—Denton Hall, near Newcastle, Tyne and Wear

Old Barbery, also referred to as 'Silky', because she appears in a rustling white gown, seems to be a benevolent ghost. There are two rooms at Denton Hall with a ghostly reputation, though Old Barbery haunts nowhere in particular and without regularity. Sometimes she manifests herself by noise only—thumping noises and footsteps, and, once, the sound of dragging, as if pulling something heavy. A confused legend is repeated in the village about a lovely girl strangled by her jealous sister at the Hall, but there is no evidence to connect Old Barbery with grisly murder.

Mrs Barnes—Littlecote, Wiltshire

In the Berkshire village of Great Shefford, where she lived, this midwife was better known as Mother Barnes. One night, in 1575, she was taken blindfolded to Littlecote Manor, home of 'Wicked' Will Darrell, where one of Darrell's mistresses, masked to hide her identity, was in the last stage of labour. The midwife helped to deliver a baby boy which Darrell immediately snatched up and flung on the fire, pushing the infant further into the blaze with his boot, as Mother Barnes begged him to stop. The frantic woman was paid off in gold and threatened with death if she uttered a word to anyone. She was tormented by her conscience for fourteen years before telling the local magistrate about the events of that terrible night, events which have never been allowed to fade into obscurity by the ghosts of midwife, mother and infant. All have been seen at various times in the bedroom and on the landing, Mother Barnes kneeling as though pleading with someone standing by the fireplace.

Elizabeth Barton—Greyfriars, London

At twenty-eight, Elizabeth Barton, the 'Holy Maid of Kent', was hanged at Tyburn, on the orders of Henry VIII. Since an illness in her teens, she had developed religious mania and, after becoming a nun at twenty-one, made several startling prophesies, one of which was that the King would die within seven months of marrying Anne Boleyn. For that she was charged with high treason and condemned. Her restless spirit not only haunts the City churchyard of Greyfriars, where she was buried in 1534, but reputedly appears as a faceless figure near to a Peckham pub, The Nun's Head, named after her.

William Batt—Oakwell Hall, Birstall, West Yorkshire

Twenty-six-year-old William Batt, eldest son of the family living at Oakwell in the 1660s, is the ghost which walks the corridors of this charming Tudor house. He was murdered, a few days before Christmas 1684, while on a visit to London. The night he died, his family, believing him to be in London until Christmas Eve, were amazed to see him enter the great hall and mount the stairs to the main bedroom, without a word to anyone. They noted how pallid he looked and on the stairs found a footprint in wet blood. Yet, in the bedroom, they could find no sign of him. Not till next day did they hear of his death at Barnet at the hand of a man named Graeme.

Ghost of Beachy Head—Eastbourne, Sussex

Beachy Head, the 500ft high chalk headland on the Sussex coast, was a medieval place of execution. Men were flung to their death from the cliff top as punishment for their crimes, often without trial. One such victim is supposed to haunt this beauty spot, which has a notorious reputation as a place for suicides, claiming an average of ten victims a year. The ghost is said to be that of a bearded priest who fled during the Dissolution of the Monasteries. He hid in a nearby farm, but was betrayed to Thomas Cromwell's men who showed no mercy. He is believed to have put a curse on the Head as he was dragged in shackles to the edge.

Lady Beauclark—Speke Hall, Liverpool, Merseyside

The White Lady of Speke is accepted as the wife of one of the Beauclarks, later owners of this sixteenth-century 'magpie' manor, originally built by the Norris family. Though the Beauclarks (descended from an illegitimate son of Charles II and Nell Gwynn) never actually resided at the Hall, they often visited. During one stay, Topham Beauclark, son of Lord 'Worthless' Sydney, is said to have announced his financial ruin. Lady Beauclark, weak from childbirth and quite distraught at this news, killed herself in the great hall, after throwing her child from a window of the Tapestry Room, the place she is seen to haunt.

Thomas à Becket—Hastings, Sussex

The martyred Becket haunts the ruined castle at Hastings where he spent some time as Dean of the church college. But why he is said to gallop through the Devon village of Lapford, at midnight on St John's Eve, is a mystery. He is supposedly on his way to Nymet Tracey, where Sir William de Tracey is reputed to have built a church as penance for his part in the murder of St Thomas. In the crypt of Canterbury Cathedral, a partly obliterated wall-painting of a mitred figure has left traces, popularly known as 'Becket's Ghost'.

Abe Beer—Milton Coombe, Devon

Old Abe Beer was once the landlord of the village pub, the Who'd Have Thought It inn. His ghostly presence has been felt from the very first night the new landlord and his wife moved in, though it is doubtful if he is responsible for the ringing of the service bell in the empty bar. That may be the prank of the phantom cavalier, described, by those who have seen him sitting on the end of a bed, as 'sad-eyed, with chestnut hair falling to his shoulders and dressed in a wine-coloured top-coat'.

'Flasker' Beesley—Staplehurst, Kent

Beesley was a smuggler, one of the notorious Goudhurst gang. He died in a battle with the revenue men, though not as dramatically as his leader, who was hurled from the church tower. Beesley's ghost has been seen at a Staplehurst farmhouse where it is said to flit across a room to escape up the chimney of the inglenook, just as he did in the old days when the King's men were after him.

Lydia Bell—St Nicholas Street, Scarborough, North Yorkshire

This daughter of a respected York confectioner was found strangled on Scarborough Sands in 1804. She was holidaying in the town and the street in which she and her parents were staying has since been haunted by Lydia Bell's ghost, walking abroad in the pink gown she wore on the night of her death. A Scarborough artist, who painted a view of the rear of the old mansion house, included Lydia in her pink dress, explaining her as the ghost his grandfather spoke of seeing regularly when he lived in the building.

Father Benedictus—Westminster Abbey, London

Father Benedictus is tall and thin, has a sallow skin and a domed head. He has deep-set, brown eyes, large and penetrating, his lips are thin, his nose distinctly hooked. He is said to walk in the cloisters of Westminster Abbey each evening between five and six o'clock. According to legend, he was stabbed to death by thieves who robbed the Chapel of the Pyx in 1303, taking the Crown Jewels and the King's treasure, worth £100,000.

Near the Tomb of the Unknown Warrior, another of the Abbey's ghosts has been seen, that of a khaki-clad soldier of World War I, mudstained and bareheaded.

Jeremy Bentham—University College, London

Jeremy Bentham was an eighteenth-century eccentric whose ghost is reputed to haunt University College, of which he was a founder. An advocate of mummification, his own mummified body, dressed in his own clothes, can be seen at the College in a moth-proof, glass-sided case. He sits holding Dapple, the walking-stick that was his lifetime companion, and which people have heard tap, tap, tapping as his ghost approaches. Those who have actually seen Bentham's ghost say he not only has his stick, but also the white gloves he would never go without.

Derek Bentley—Colliers Wood, London

Derek Bentley was nineteen when he was hanged in 1953, for the murder of Constable Sidney Miles during a gun fight on the roof of a Croydon warehouse. His accomplice, who fired the fatal shot, was only sixteen at the time and too young to hang. Since the morning he died for a murder he did not commit, the presence of Derek Bentley has seemingly been active, constantly haunting his family.

In recent years, the ghost of Bentley's father has also been seen, according to the family. He died in 1974, still campaigning to clear his son's name.

Sir Bertram of Bothal—Warkworth Castle, Northumberland

A despairing ghost is that of Sir Bertram of Bothal, who fought with Lord (Hotspur) Percy of Alnwick against the Scots, proving himself fearless in battle. How then did such a brave knight end his days as the sorrowing Hermit of Warkworth, living in a cave above the River Coquet, where his ghost is said still to haunt? His bright hopes of marrying Isobel, daughter of Lord Widdrington, were crushed by a double tragedy which drove him to a life of mourning: unwittingly he killed Isobel and his own brother, who was disguised as a Scot, while attempting to rescue the girl from captivity.

The Bettiscombe Skull—near Bridport, Dorset

For years, almost a century in fact, this skull at Bettiscombe House, has been considered one of the screaming variety. To remove it from the farmhouse is reckoned to mean death to the person who touches it. Apart from this, it could cause unlimited disturbance to house and household, which would only subside when it was put back in its rightful place. Why so is a mystery, as much a mystery as to whose skull it is. Legend claims it is the head of a negro slave, purchased in the West Indies in 1765 by John Pinney. Named 'Old Bettiscombe', he came to England in 1880, when his master returned to end his days in Dorset. Or is it a skull dug out of an ancient barrow on the nearby downs? Perhaps the professor from the Royal College of Surgeons is right when he says it's nothing more romantic than a normal European skull of a woman in her late twenties, who died in the house after a long period of close confinement.

Other skulls with supernatural attributes are to be found at: Affetside, Lancashire; Brougham Hall, Cumbria; Threlkeld Place, Cumbria; Turton Tower, Lancashire, and Warbleton Priory Farm, Sussex.

Lady de Bevere—Skipsea Castle, Humberside

She is one of the most enduring ghosts on record, having haunted the castle, now no more than a great mound of earth, since Norman times. In fact, Lady de Bevere was a niece of William the Conqueror, and was married to Drogo de Bevere after the Battle of Hastings, where he fought so fearlessly that William rewarded him with both Skipsea and his niece. But Drogo, the tough, bold soldier, was a cruel and brutal husband, so much so that he killed his wife when she would no longer submit to his savage demands. Drogo fled the country and the White Lady of Skipsea began a thousand years of haunting on Albermarle Hill.

Alice Birch—Goodrich Castle, Herefordshire

Alice Birch, and her betrothed, a Royalist sympathiser named Clifford, took refuge in Goodrich Castle while Colonel Birch, Alice's Roundhead uncle, had it under attack in the May of 1646. The monotony of the long siege, and hopelessness of their personal situation, caused them to decide to escape through the Parliamentary lines. Once across the River Wye there would be no stopping them. But the river, in full spate, put an end to their dreams, sweeping both them and their mount to death, a tragic moment which, many times since, has been re-enacted by a spectral Alice and her lover.

The Black Canon—Bolton Abbey, North Yorkshire

The Augustinian canon who haunts at Bolton is the best documented of all the Yorkshire ghosts and probably the best known. Though it has been seen frequently over the years since before World War I, the Marquis of Hartington's eye-witness account, published in 1936 in *Lord Halfax's Ghost Book*, remains one of the most detailed descriptions:

> '... an old man of 65 or so ... face unusually round ... heavily lined and wrinkled ... eyes bright ... the face might have been that of an old woman but for ... a week's growth of greyish stubble on the chin.'

King George V's interest in this haunting was such that he was one of the three distinguished signatories who witnessed Lord Hartington's account of what he saw on the Sunday night of 18 August 1912.

The Black Horse—Scarborough, North Yorkshire

The Black Horse of Scarborough has been part of Yorkshire folklore for close on 800 years. It began in the twelfth century, with reports of a huge black horse seen galloping near to the town. Hundreds claimed to have seen it and their accounts seldom varied—as the riderless animal passed, the sky blackened and there was a violent thunderstorm accompanied by hailstones. After nearly a year of these reports, farm workers on the cliffs said they saw the horse gallop to the edge, leap into the sea and disappear, after which the usual storm raged. Hoof marks of the great black charger remained on the cliff top for all of the following year.

Trumpet Major Blandford—Tarrant Hinton, Dorset

Blandford, a trumpet major in the dragoons and a spare-time poacher, lost a hand in a violent skirmish with gamekeepers defending the deer of the Cranborne Chase. The 'battle' between keepers and poachers took place on Chettle Common on the night of 16 December 1780. On both sides, several men were severely wounded and one of the keepers later died. Blandford recovered, went to London, and was eventually buried there. But a ghostly hand, thought to be Blandford's, which was buried in Pimperne churchyard, Dorset, has been seen over the years near Tarrant Hinton, seeking unity with the body to which it belongs.

Mary Blandy—Henley on Thames, Oxfordshire

Mary Blandy is Henley's best known ghost. She was a local girl who poisoned her father when he objected to her plans to marry a man of whom he disapproved. Since her trial in Oxford, and subsequent hanging in 1752, her ghost has meandered around, walking beside the river, in the graveyard, and standing under an old mulberry tree in the garden of the house where she lived. Once it was seen at Henley's Kenton Theatre, standing at the back of the stalls as if watching a performance of *The Hanging Tree*, a play based on Mary Blandy's crime.

Lady de Blenkinsopp—Blenkinsopp Castle, Northumberland

Although Lady Blenkinsopp's ghost is described as a White Lady, she was, in reality, the dusky-skinned wife Sir Bryan de Blenkinsopp brought home from the Crusade. Hopefully, she haunts the castle ruins awaiting the return of Sir Bryan, who went back to the Holy War in high dudgeon after they had quarrelled vehemently about her dowry. According to the best legends, she correctly accused him of marrying her only for the marriage settlement of gold and jewels, which she buried out of spite, in some inaccessable place beneath the castle. Perhaps, say some, it is the treasure her ghost is seeking, to ease her conscience.

Queen Boadicea (The Cammeringham Light)—Lincolnshire

Some who have seen this phenomenon, locally known as 'The Cammeringham Light', say they have seen Queen Boadicea driving her chariot. What they see speeding towards them, out of the early morning mists, certainly looks like that—a woman in a long, billowing gown, her hair streaming behind her as she whips up a pair of horses pulling the chariot in which she stands. This happens only at Cammeringham, a small village a few miles north of Lincoln on the B1398 which runs parallel to the old Roman Ermine Street, territory over which Queen Boadicea must surely have travelled.

The restless spirits of Queen Boadicea and her two daughters wander near the ancient earthworks of Ambresbury, on the Epping road. Hereabouts, according to tradition, they took poison so as not to become prisoners of the Romans, following the defeat of Boadicea's army in AD 62.

Boatswain—Newstead Abbey, near Linby, Nottinghamshire

When Lord Byron lived at Newstead Abbey in the 1800s, he had a pet Newfoundland dog named Boatswain, reputed to haunt the ruined abbey church, near the site of the high altar which is where the poet gave it a fit and proper burial. From the time Sir John Byron bought and restored the Abbey, in 1540, the family was troubled by ill-luck, and the ghost of a Black Friar, whose appearance preceded each misfortune.

Queen Anne (Boleyn)—The Tower of London

The busiest ghost in all England is, without doubt, Anne Boleyn, who laid her pretty head on the block on 19 May 1536, less than three years after her coronation as Henry's queen. Anne is a circulating ghost, reputed to walk at the Tower of London, as well as at Hampton Court, Hever Castle, Old Blickling Hall and Salle Church in Norfolk, Rochford Hall, Bollin Hall, and even Windsor Castle. Of all these haunts, the Tower is where she has been seen most frequently and where the sighting is officially on record. At Hever, where Henry courted her, she appears as a happy ghost, while at Blickling she is at her most bizarre—a decapitated figure riding in a coach with a bloodied head resting in her lap. The coach is pulled by four headless horses, driven by a headless coachman, said to be her father, Sir Thomas Boleyn.

Lady Mary Bolles—Old Heath Hall, Wakefield, West Yorkshire

Though the old hall is a ruin and the ghost of old Lady Mary is fast fading, the legends about this seventeenth-century eccentric live on. Most of her life she lived well, so, when she died, at eighty-three, she did that in style too. She left £400 for her actual funeral, £700 for mourning and £120 for hospitality to allcomers wishing to pay their last respects during the six weeks she specified must elapse before her burial.

Lady Boston—Boston Manor House, Brentford, London, W5

Some who work at Boston Manor talk of a ghost, believed to be that of Lady Boston, who died in 'mysterious circumstances', after his Lordship found her in the arms of a lover. Legend has it he killed her in a jealous rage and buried the body somewhere in the manor grounds, today the gardens of the National Institute of Housecraft. Her skeleton, found by nuns some years later, was reinterred under what is now an ivy-covered mound. Both staff and visitors report sighting a shadowy female figure, which disappears near a giant cypress tree where the lovers met.

William Boulter—Salisbury Plain, Wiltshire

Boulter was a highwayman who, like most of that ilk, died young—aged thirty. He was born at Poulshot, near Devizes, in 1748, and made the long drop at Winchester in the summer of 1778. Salisbury Plain is where his ghost is mostly seen, particularly when the nights are moonless and stormy. He is said also to haunt stretches of the A30, as well as the old road to Bath where the coach trade was at its briskest. Possibly he is the phantom highwayman heard—and sometimes seen—galloping furiously through Marlborough.

John Bradshaw—Westminster Abbey, London

John Bradshaw presided at the 'High Court of Justice' which tried and condemned Charles I in 1649. It was he who signed the death warrant which sent the King to the scaffold on the morning of 30 January. He signed it in the Inslip Rooms of the Deanery at Westminster Abbey, rooms he occupied during the Commonwealth, and the place his ghost is said to haunt. Heavy footsteps heard in the passage and on the stairs at dead of night are supposedly his, since that is where his ghost is reported to have been seen. It has also been seen in Red Lion Square, walking arm in arm with two other spectral figures—Oliver Cromwell and General Ireton.

Babes of Bramber—near Shoreham, Sussex

The children of William de Broase, friend of the Conqueror and Norman lord of Bramber Castle, are the pathetic ghosts of this Sussex downland village. A thin, ragged boy and girl are still to be seen fleetingly gazing towards the castle ruins, or begging for food. They were innocent victims of the ruthlessness of King John who, suspecting de Broase of plotting, demanded the children's custody as proof of his loyalty. Though the family fled to Ireland, the children were arrested and brought back to Windsor, where they were starved to death in the castle dungeons.

John Breed—Rye, Sussex

Even if the ghost of John Breed, an eighteenth-century butcher, is rarely, if ever, seen these days, his skull can still be viewed in Rye Town Hall. So can the iron cage in which he was gibbeted for fifty years. His crime was premeditated murder. In 1743, he killed Allan Grebell in St Mary's Churchyard, stabbing him in the back with his butcher's knife. As he struck, he believed he was killing James Lamb, a Rye magistrate who, that week, had fined Breed for giving short weight. It was a twist of fate that Lamb had stayed at home that night to attend to other matters, having got his friend, Grebell, to see an acquaintance sail on the evening tide.

There is a haunted room at Rye's Mermaid Inn where spectral duellists are seen in the night, fighting to the death of one of them, whose body the victor then bundles into an oubliette.

The Bridesmaids of Great Melton, Norfolk

Of all the phantom coaches that haunt the highways—and there are very many—this one has a quartet of the loveliest ghosts as passengers. They are lovely, that is, if they still have their heads on their shoulders. If they haven't, they are a grisly spectacle which spells trouble for those who see it. These are the ghosts of four bridesmaids who, returning from a wedding on an ink-black night, got no further than Great Melton. That is where, periodically, a phantom coach and horses plunges recklessly into the night, seemingly in the hands of a drunken coachman who, all those years ago, ran off the road into a deep pool, drowning himself and his passengers.

Sir Barney Brograve—Waxham, Norfolk

Sir Barney is only one of seven ghosts to haunt Waxham. All are Brograves, a family which stretches back over the centuries to the Crusades. All died warring, except Sir Barney, who died 'a bad old bachelor'. One New Year's Eve, shortly before he joined the others, he gave a party at the Old Hall, to which the six ghostly knights, Sirs Ralph, Edmund, John, Francis, Thomas and Charles were invited and their toasts drunk.

Emily Brontë—Wadsworth Moor, Haworth, West Yorkshire

Emily Jane Brontë wrote of Cathy Earnshaw's ghost haunting the moors, seeking Heathcliff, in much the same way as the ghost of Emily herself is said to haunt the wild, wind-torn moorland which she loved so much. She haunts alone, her head down as if in thought, walking a narrow path leading to a little waterfall which was the sisters' favourite place and within sight of High Withens, the lonely brooding house Emily made into *Wuthering Heights*.

Rupert Chawner Brooke—Grantchester, Cambridgeshire

The unexplained footsteps heard moving through the garden of the old vicarage at Grantchester are generally accepted as those of Rupert Brooke, the soldier-poet returning, spectrally speaking, to the house and garden he loved and made the subject of one of his most famous poems, 'The Old Vicarage, Grantchester'.

Edward Broome—Keresley, Warwickshire

It is 450 years since the Corley farmer, Edward Broome, was hanged in the barn at Penny Park Farm. Today Penny Park is built over and the barn is a community centre, yet still reputed to be haunted by the vengeance-seeking spectre of Broome, whose murder was made to look like suicide. The man who hanged him, John Shaw, was in love with Squire Sadler's daughter, Elizabeth, as was Broome who went to almost any length to get a glimpse of her, even to stopping her carriage on the roads around Coventry. In one such hold-up, he struggled with the coachman causing his pistol to go off, accidentally hitting Elizabeth. Within minutes of hearing of this mishap, an enraged Shaw, thinking the worst, sought out Edward Broome—and his favourite retriever—and killed them both.

Theophilus Broome—Chilton Cantelo, Somerset

Broome was a Civil War veteran, whose skull has been preserved at Higher Chilton Farm for more than 300 years. One of his last requests, when he died in 1670, was that his head be removed and kept in the farmhouse, presumably to prevent it being hacked off and publicly displayed, one of the barbaric things done to Parliamentarian supporters during the Restoration. Whenever there has been any attempt to inter the skull, Broome's ghost has shown his displeasure by making life uncomfortable for the persons wanting to bury it.

Bella Brown—Druridge Bay, Northumberland

Bella lived at Cresswell, where the rocks around Snab Point have been the graveyard of countless sailing ships driven ashore by the merciless North Sea. One such was the *Gustav* which Bella saw go aground. She ran for five miles in the gathering dusk to call the lifeboat at Newbiggin and that mid-nineteenth-century drama has left behind a durable haunting on the shores of Druridge Bay where Bella's spectre is seen in the twilight, clambering breathlessly over the dunes to get help. Some say a spectral dog runs with her, though that is more likely to be the companion of another of the long bay's ghosts—an old crone, from Widdrington, who was trapped by the tide, gathering mussels. Overlooking the sands is Cresswell Tower, ghosted by a white lady of Saxon origin.

Lilly Browne—Stepney, London

For twenty-six years Mrs Lillian Browne was matron at Thames Magistrates Court in Stepney. Only because of ill-health did she give up the job, in the winter of 1970. When she died, seven weeks later, she was aged seventy-seven. Extraordinary incidents in the last few months of 1976 convinced Court staff, and a medium called in to investigate, that Mrs Browne's ghost had returned to keep a spectral eye on proceedings.

Marion de la Bruere—Ludlow Castle, Shropshire

The ghost of Marion has been re-enacting her death dive from Pendower Tower of Ludlow Castle since the latter half of the twelfth century. She was the headstrong, lovesick young daughter of one of the defenders of the Castle, who foolishly lowered a rope and encouraged Arnold de Lys, a young soldier of the besieging army to climb up into her tower room. Only when she saw other soldiers, a hundred at least, follow Arnold commando-style up the rope and into the castle did she realise what she had done—impregnable Ludlow was in enemy hands because of her stupidity. Dazed and sickened by the thought, she seized her lover's sword as he lay sleeping and sank it into his chest, then ran to the battlements and jumped, screaming, into the night.

Lord Buckhurst—Old Swan, Battersea, London

Lord Buckhurst who, in Restoration times, lodged at the Old Swan, overlooking the river at Battersea, lured Nell Gwynn not only from the stage to become his mistress, but also from the bed of King Charles, and that in itself was no mean feat. Pepys, on hearing the gossip, wrote in his diary, 'Poor girl! I pity her'. Twentieth-century diarists have pity for his lordship's ghost having still to haunt the Old Swan, since it was rebuilt in the 1960s in modern style.

Marmaduke Buckle—Goodramgate, York

Marmaduke was a crippled boy who lived with his family in a house in Goodramgate, in seventeenth-century York. The house is still there and so is young Buckle's ghost, switching on lights, opening doors and making his presence felt on the creaking old staircase. Scratched on the plaster of an upstairs room are the words: 'Marmaduke Buckle 1697–1715', presumably the year of his birth and the year when the torment of his disability caused him to hang himself from one of the roof timbers.

A short walk away, in Gray's Court, is Treasurer's House, where a plumber's apprentice, now a policeman, once saw a group of ghostly Roman soldiers march through the cellar in which he was working, in the early 1950s.

John Buckstone—Haymarket Theatre, London

John Baldwin Buckstone spurned a naval career, failed to make the grade as a solicitor's clerk, so joined a company of strolling players to become one of the great names of the Victorian stage, as actor and playwright. In 1853 he became manager of London's Haymarket Theatre and has remained there ever since, staying on to haunt the place after his death in 1879. Among theatre personalities who have encountered his ghost in recent years are Dame Flora Robson, Dame Margaret Rutherford, Meriel Forbes (Lady Richardson), Drusilla Wills, Victor Leslie, and Mrs Stuart Wilson, Chairman and Managing Director of the theatre.

Louisa Bunting—Debham, Suffolk

Louisa Bunting died suddenly in 1879, just four months after her wedding day. She was found dead on the floor of the room in which she used to sleep while visiting her sister Miss Bees, who lived in Debham's curving main street. Miss Bees saw her sister's ghost in that little house, and particularly in that room, for many years afterwards. Possibly Louisa Bunting still haunts today—a youngish woman, sometimes sitting with an arm resting on the table, and on her left cheek a red weal which happened when she fell and struck her face.

Clara Burnett—Usk, Monmouthshire

Clara Burnett died, broken-hearted, more than 200 years ago, a delicate creature callously imprisoned in the Cross Keys Inn, at Usk, to prevent her meeting her lover. Her tormented soul continues to haunt the bedroom where she is said to have cried herself to death in the 600-year-old pub. Although members of a local spiritualist society gave this ghost an identity in 1960, there are still those who do not accept that it is Clara Burnett who haunts. Some say it is the ghost of a grossly disfigured girl who was never allowed to leave her bedroom prison because of her horrific disability.

Thomas Busby—Sandhutton, North Yorkshire

The ghost seen in Sandhutton, with lolling head and hangman's noose still knotted around the throat, is that of Tom Busby, hanged and gibbeted in 1702 for killing his father-in-law. After he'd married the daughter of Daniel Auty, a counterfeiter, he became the old man's partner, until they rowed about how the money should be shared. Busby lost his temper, seized a hammer and beat Auty to death. The gallows, on which Busby's body was left to rot, stood at the crossroads opposite the Busby Stoop Inn, where the present landlord keeps a chair reserved for the ghost which haunts also in the pub.

2nd Marquess of Bute—Cardiff Castle, Glamorgan

The man who has been Custodian of Cardiff Castle for fifteen years is convinced it is haunted—by the ghosts of a man and a young woman in a long robe, both of whom he has seen. The man is believed to be the 2nd Marquess of Bute, whose family owned the castle for six generations. After a glittering banquet, he died quite suddenly, in the little dressing-room he used, behind what is now the castle library. The room has been converted into a small chapel in which a bust of the Marquess stands on the spot where he died, while his ghost walks the library.

Squire Butler—Barnwell, Cambridgeshire

Jacob Butler was 6ft 4in tall, which earned him the title 'the Giant Squire'. He was a barrister, the oldest in England at the time he died, in 1766. Why his ghost returned to the Old Abbey House at Barnwell is a mystery, but, until recent years, there were reports that he did haunt there, although he was not the only supernatural resident.

There was also the figure of a white nun who, it was said, used an underground passage from the old nunnery (now Jesus College) to reach Barnwell, to meet her lover, a monk. When her sin was revealed she was walled up alive.

Dr Butts—Corpus Christi, Cambridge

During the plague year of 1630, Dr Butts was Vice Chancellor as well as Master of Corpus Christi. Students, as much as the townsfolk of Cambridge, suffered disastrously, which drove the doctor to become frantic with worry. So much so, he hanged himself by his garters, in the Old Lodge, since when his ghost has frequented the college.

He does not haunt alone, however. He shares Old Lodge with the ghost of a student, surreptitiously courting the daughter of Dr Spencer, another seventeenth-century Master of Christi. Surprised during a clandestine meeting with the girl, in the small hours, her student-lover squeezed himself into a kitchen cupboard, was trapped and suffocated.

Admiral John Byng—Greenwich, London

Admiral Byng died, frock-coated and bewigged, kneeling blindfold on a cushion, facing a firing squad. This son of Lord Torrington, who entered the Navy as a boy of fourteen, was unjustly shot in March 1757 for failure to engage the French fleet and save Minorca. From August 1756, until court-marshalled in December, he was kept under arrest in a small room in what is today the Royal Naval College at Greenwich. There his ghost is active, sometimes a vague figure 'floating' in the corridors, at other times an unseen presence flinging open doors, beyond which there is nothing but the sound of footsteps retreating into the distance.

Best known of the ghosts of Greenwich are the two cowled figures on the Tulip Staircase of the seventeenth-century Queen's House, now part of the National Maritime Museum. A Canadian clergyman photographed them in 1966, while touring England. His picture is in the files of the Ghost Club, whose president, Peter Underwood, investigated the case and reported on it in his book *A Host of Hauntings*.

Elizabeth Bynge—All Cannings, Wiltshire

'A ghost with the sweetest of faces' is how the Grey Lady of All Cannings Rectory has been described. She is thought to be Elizabeth Bynge, wife of the Reverend Robert Bynge, the Royalist rector, who built the house in 1646. With her three sons, all under six years, she was evicted from the rectory by Cromwell's men, yet, if it is she, her ghost still lingers there, passing along an upstairs corridor, visiting at least two of the bedrooms, and using the long-removed spiral staircase to go, via the old kitchen, into the garden.

C

Sir Walter Calverley—Calverley Hall, West Yorkshire

In a fit of insane frenzy, Walter Calverley very nearly succeeded in killing all his family. After drinking and gambling away his inheritance, he accused his wife of infidelity and stabbed her and two of his sons. He then rode off to find his other son, intent on killing him. However, after a few miles, his horse threw him and he was arrested. Sir Walter was eventually convicted of murdering only the two children, since his wife was saved from death by her steel corsets. He was sentenced to be pressed to death with stones and weights piled on his chest. Since suffering that terrible fate, his ghost has been encountered, galloping near to Calverley Hall on a headless horse.

Lady Frederick Campbell—Coombe Bank, Sunridge, Kent

Lady Campbell burned to ashes in a fire at Coombe Bank in 1807. The only part of her recovered was a small piece of one thumb, which her ghost has been searching for ever since. The blaze was thought to be the fulfilment of a curse put on her by her first husband, Lord Ferrers, hanged in 1760 for murdering his steward who had given evidence against him in divorce proceedings brought by her ladyship. Before he died he cursed his wife to suffer a worse death than his.

Kitty Canham—Thorpe-le-Soken, Essex

Kitty Canham lies in the churchyard at Thorpe, next door to the Bell Inn, in the High Street. Wedded in the 1700s to the then vicar of Thorpe, she grew tired of village life and went to London. Within weeks she met and bigamously married Lord Dalmeny who, completely unaware of the circumstances, took his new bride to live in Verona. When near to death some three years later, Kitty confessed her past and got his lordship to promise she would be buried in her own village. This was done, her forgiving 'husbands' helping to carry her coffin to the grave. Her ghost—'a rather shadowy female figure, leaving a white glow'—is thought to haunt The Bell, on occasions even using the spare beds in the hotel's guest rooms.

Giles Cannard—Shepton Mallet, Somerset

Cannard was an innkeeper who acted as middle-man for the highwaymen and ruffians of the West Country roads. He did business, too, with the smuggling gangs from Bridgewater Bay. But, greedy for more, he took to forgery and that was his undoing. When the law caught up with him, he hanged himself and was buried at the crossing of five roads, a mile south of Shepton, where his footpads used to ambush travellers. That is the place where his ghost lurks today, outside the inn which bears his name.

Brother Cantata—Rye, Sussex

This brother, who had a fine singing voice, was walled up in Rye's fourteenth-century friary for planning to elope to France with a pretty girl who lived next door to the Augustinian community. It is said he died, demented, gobbling like a turkey. Indeed, there are some who believe Rye's Turkey Cock Lane is so called because, since his death, ghostly gobblings have been heard in that vicinity. Yet his ghost—a tall, cowled figure—did not appear demented when seen in the chapel garden, or, more recently, in the guesthouse behind the old monastery building.

Brother Cantata is not alone in his haunting. There have been reports of seven ghostly, cowled figures moving across the chapel garden and dissolving into the surrounding wall. They are thought to be shades of the friars of Rye who suffered an horrific death when the monasteries were sacked on the orders of Henry VIII. They were buried alive, standing up.

The Captain—Dolphin Tavern, Penzance, Cornwall

Local regulars call this ghost of an old seafaring character 'Captain George', though one can only make a guess as to his history. He is seen wearing a tricorn hat, lace ruffles and a coat with brass buttons, which suggests somebody of rank. He is most probably a captain off one of the fleet of sailing ships that used to put into Mounts Bay in Elizabethan days. Though the Dolphin is a waterside tavern, and once the hide of smugglers, it is doubtful if Captain George was ever engaged in rum-running—not in all that finery.

Maude Carew—Bury St Edmunds, Suffolk

The Grey Lady of Bury St Edmunds is reputed to be Maude Carew, the nun thought to have poisoned Humphrey, Duke of Gloucester, during his imprisonment in 1447. Some believed his death was from natural causes, though many were convinced his arch-enemy, William, Earl of Suffolk, had him murdered. Supposedly the crime was committed where Maude's wraith walks, in the houses built into the ruined west front of the Abbey church. Hereabouts, shades of some of the former Abbey monks have been reported.

Billie Carleton—Savoy Hill, London

This is one of the BBC hauntings, in fact the first. Edwardian actress Billie Carleton, who died on returning to her flat after a Victory Ball in November 1918, left a ghost which haunted the BBC's first home at Savoy Hill, off Strand. The old 2LO building was housed in a block of converted flats, one of which had been Billie Carleton's. The door to the flat, later used as an office, used to open silently and inexplicably, so that staff at once became aware of the unseen presence.

Other BBC ghosts include the tall figure of a bewhiskered butler carrying a tray, who limps along the corridors of Broadcasting House, and the man in Room 33 of the old Langham Hotel

—now the BBC staff club—believed to be a German officer who leapt to his death from a fourth-floor window.

Joan Carn—Withycombe, Somerset

Joan Carn was a witch, born at Sandhill, a beautiful Elizabethan manor house near Withycombe. She murdered three husbands, and herself died from drowning after being flung into a pond. There is a brass plate to her in Withycombe Church, where she is said to haunt and where she was supposedly buried in 1612. Supposedly? While there is certainly an ancient tombstone bearing her name and mourners saw her coffin buried, they returned from the funeral to find her at home frying bacon and eggs!

Lady Louisa Carteret—Longleat, Wiltshire

Lady Louisa, the second Viscountess Weymouth, is by far the most spectacular of Longleat's phantoms. A portrait of her in a lime green dress shows her as a beauty of her day. But the lovely Louisa was unfaithful to her husband. She daringly smuggled her lover into Longleat and they were discovered together by the Viscount. In the duel that followed, the Countess's lover was cut down and his body buried in the cellars. Louisa's grief has kept her ghost haunting the Green Lady's corridor and the Monmouth Stairs periodically ever since. Some years ago, the bones and boots of a man were found beneath the cellar floor.

Queen Catherine (of Aragon) Buckden, Huntingdonshire

Henry VIII was wedded to Catherine of Aragon for twenty-three years. After his marriage to Anne Boleyn, he banished Queen Kate to Buckden Palace, where the local people took her to their hearts, even going to her defence with sticks and pitch forks when the King sent the Duke of Suffolk to move her to Fotheringhay Castle. Reluctantly, she went to nearby Kimbolton the year after, but, when she died there in 1536, it was to Buckden (now a monastery) her wraith returned, haunting, it is said, the little room behind the chapel.

The Cavaliers of Marston Moor, North Yorkshire

Like the Unknown Warrior of World War I these ghosts of the battle of Marston Moor are nameless, though they are identifiable by their long cloaks, their wide-brimmed hats with cockades, their shoulder-length hair and high top boots, as remnants of the Cavalier army routed by the Parliamentarians. Four thousand Royalist soldiers were slain in that summer-evening battle of 1644, and these are undoubtedly spectral flashbacks of that terrible day, though usually no more than three or four dazed, bewildered men are seen stumbling along at the roadside, presumably intent on escaping the wrath of the pursuing Roundheads.

Abbot Chard—Forde Abbey, Dorset

Thomas Chard was the last of the Abbots of Forde. He restored and beautified the Abbey, building the vaulted cloister and the great rectory, before he and his twelve Cistercian monks were thrown out when Henry VIII ordered the Dissolution of the Monasteries. Although he died peacefully, in 1544, as Vicar of Thorncombe, his ghost has not rested, returning to Forde from time to time, to walk in his great hall, particularly near the high table.

King Charles I—Windsor, Berkshire

Charles I, whose decapitated body was taken to Windsor for burial, is believed to be the ghost which walks in the Canon's House, in the castle precincts. Those who have seen it say there is no doubt it is the Martyr King, the features being remarkably like those in the famous Van Dyck portrait. A headless phantom, seen at Marple Hall in Cheshire, is said to be that of the King, also, though why he should appear there is not clear.

Aunt Charlotte—Bryanston House, Dorset

Aunt Charlotte was one of the Portman family who lived at Bryanston. She sat for Gainsborough, and his portrait of her is in the National Portrait Gallery. But not her ghost: that used to haunt the old Portman home, near Blandford, although it seems to have ceased walking since the house was pulled down and Bryanston School built in its stead. It is reputed that a phantom version of the Portman family coach is sometimes seen at full moon, making its way up the drive leading to the house.

Darkie Chase—Royal Castle Hotel, Dartmouth, Devon

Darkie Chase was small with a malicious grin and a coffee-coloured skin. He was once an ostler at the Royal Castle in the hey-day of coach travel and lived in over the inn stables. His ghost is one of two which the late Mrs Gwyneth Powell experienced during the twenty-five or more years that she ran the hotel. Darkie Chase, 'small, like a jockey and a bit alarming', she sometimes passed on the stairs. The other manifestation was also experienced by many of her guests who were usually happy to learn that the noise they heard in the night—invariably as the nearby church clock struck 2 am—was the urgent departure of a phantom coach taking Mary of Orange to Brixham to join her husband, William.

Miser Chickett—Brushmakers' Arms, Upham, Hampshire

Brushmaking was Miser Chickett's business. He'd been in the trade a long time, hoarded every penny he made and took his money with him wherever he went. At night he slept with it under his bed in an upstairs front room of the Brushmakers' Arms. Which is where he was found battered to death, his money gone. Chickett's ghost occupies the same low-ceilinged little room in the Brushmakers', though there are some who say it's not the ghost of the miser at all, but that of a former landlord, said to have been murdered while counting the day's takings.

Lizzie Church—University College Hospital, London

The ghost of Nurse Church who, at the turn of the century, accidentally administered an overdose of morphia to her fiance, is said to appear whenever morphine injections are being given to patients at London's University College Hospital.

Elsewhere in Gower Street, not far from the hospital, people have encountered another ghost of an unidentified man with a bandaged head, dressed in 1930s' clothes. Nearby Tavistock Place has been the haunt, since mid-Victorian times, of an unnamed man in a frock coat and a stove-pipe hat hung with funeral ribbons. As he moves along, another phantom figure emerges, a nursemaid, who peers into his wan face, and runs away.

Pieman Clibbon—Datchworth, Hertfordshire

There was nothing simple about this eighteenth-century pieman with the name of Clibbon. By day he hawked his victuals in the market-place, talking with the farmers in the sale-ring, and at night he robbed those very same men as they rode home with their fat purses. When finally unmasked, Clibbon was beaten near to death, dragged several miles behind a horse to Woolmer Green, and left to die. Which accounts for this ghost, sighted in the lanes around Datchworth Green—a writhing body roped to a horse and usually accompanied by the moans of a dying man.

Rosamund Clifford—Creslow Manor, Buckinghamshire

The ghost of Creslow, thought to be Rosamund Clifford, has not been seen or heard since the 1850s. A former High Sheriff of Buckinghamshire, who had great contempt for all haunted houses, ghosts and apparitions, spent a restless night in what was termed the 'haunted room', a small room above the crypt. Although he did not see anything, he was repeatedly disturbed by the loud rustling of a stiff silk dress and a woman's footsteps. The Cliffords occupied twelfth-century Creslow in Stuart times, Sir Thomas Clifford having leased the property after the Restoration in 1660.

Jane Maria Clousen—Kidbrooke, London

Jane Maria Clousen was attacked and left dying in Kidbrooke Lane, between Blackheath and Shooters Hill, on an April evening in 1871. A blood-covered hammer, found close by, was the clue which caused police to arrest Edmund Pook, for whose father Jane Clousen had worked as a maid. Despite formidable evidence, Pook was acquitted after producing a convincing alibi. But, years afterwards, the lane was said to be ghosted by the figure of the murdered girl, though some heard only her screams and groans. In recent years, Kidbrooke Jane—as she became known—has not been seen at all; instead a shadowy female figure in Victorian garb haunts in the vicinity of Hare and Billet Road, where, shortly before the turn of the century, a desperately unhappy wife hanged herself.

The Long Coastguardsman of Bacton, Norfolk

Except that he appears to walk tall, little is known about this spectre of the sands seen abroad on dark nights, between Bacton and Mundesley. He seems to delight in rough seas and stormy weather. When the wind is high and roaring, he sings and shouts as he wades. Sometimes he laughs wildly and at other times he calls for help, as he must have done many times when engaged in his coastguard duties. It is doubtful if he has any connection with the Happisburgh ghost, which haunts what was once a smugglers' haven, six miles to the south.

Grizelle Cochrane—Buckton, Northumberland

The ghost of Grizelle Cochrane, an eighteen-year-old Scots girl, haunts a spinney on the Great North road, 4 miles north of Belford. The place, known as 'Grizzie's Clump', is where this daring daughter of Sir John Cochrane of Ochiltree, dressed as a man, held up the London-to-Edinburgh coach to seize her father's death warrant from the royal courier. Her lone action, performed with two pistols stolen from the postman at Belford, saved her father from execution for his part in the Jacobite uprising of 1715.

Leathery Coit—Fleece Inn, Elland, West Yorkshire

Leathery Coit was a pedlar, as tough as hide after long years of travelling the moors. He kept his carriage and horses in old stables adjoining The Fleece, in Elland's Westgate, until the night he was killed. Leathery, brutally done to death in an upstairs room at The Fleece, was dragged down a flight of wooden steps, leaving a trail of blood as a permanent reminder of the crime. No amount of scrubbing can remove the stains, any more than time can remove sight or sound of Leathery's lingering ghost, furiously driving along Dog Lane, heralded by a violent rush of wind, however calm the night.

Betty Coke—Melbourne Hall, Derbyshire

The lovely Betty Coke was the daughter of the man who was Queen Anne's vice-chamberlain, Sir John Coke. He bought and restored Melbourne Hall and, when not in attendance, at Court, lived there with his family. It was there that Betty spent many hours pursuing the arts, and, in particular, working on her tapestries. She left a fine piece of tapestry incomplete when she died, and, according to tradition, her ghost returns to the Hall, periodically, to add a few stitches to her unfinished wallhanging.

Henry Coker—Hill Deverill, Wiltshire

Henry Coker was the last of the lords of the manor of Hill Deverill, near Warminster. He died in 1730 and is thought still to haunt the village where he is known as 'Old Coker'. He follows his phantom pack in a ghostly hunt, circling the parish, sometimes going through the garden of the old manor house. The sounds of the hunt—galloping horses, jingling harness, ringing spurs, voices calling, and the blowing of the horn—are all heard.

Thomas Cole—The Ostrich, Colnbrook, Buckinghamshire

A fourteenth-century innkeeper named Jarman and his wife made a rich living out of murder at Ye Old Ostrich. One can still see the cosy little bedroom which the wealthiest traveller was always given. Thomas Cole, a prosperous clothier of Reading slept there most soundly on two visits, and, on the third, went the way of fifty-nine others before him—tipped from his bed through a trap door into a boiling brewhouse vat. That way Tom Cole became strong ale and the landlord became richer on the pickings from the travellers' pockets. Tom Cole's horse, found wandering, led a suspicious servant back to the inn, causing the landlord's wife to panic into a confession. Tom Cole's ghost has since been found wandering in the inn where he came to such a sudden and scalding end.

Lady Constantia Coleraine—Bruce Castle, Tottenham, London

This ghost dates from the seventeenth century when the beautiful Lady Constantia killed herself in desperation at being locked up in the tower of Bruce Castle. Her husband, Henry, the second Baron Coleraine, was such a jealous man he could not tolerate his lovely wife being seen by other men, so kept her confined to her room, the door locked whenever he went away. On 3 November 1680, she took her baby and threw herself screaming from the gallery of the 30ft tower to the courtyard below, a drama which left behind an anniversary haunting, complete with screams.

Sam Collins—Islington Green, London

He was an Irishman called Vagg who took the name Collins when he began touring the halls as the Singing Chimney Sweep. In the 1860s, he opened what was to become one of Victorian London's most famous places of entertainment, Collins Music Hall, facing Islington Green. Fire destroyed most of it a hundred years later, leaving only the bar, the old façade, and Sam's ghost, which shared the haunt with a spectral Dan Leno who occasionally turned up at rehearsals, and continued a lifetime habit of snapping his fingers in disapproval of an act.

William Constable—Burton Constable Hall, near Hull, Humberside

Is it any wonder that William Constable haunts his old home, since he was the man who, in the 1850s, did more than any previous owner to turn the original Elizabethan hall into a comfortable and magnificent home? A woman occupant of the Gold Bedroom woke one night to see a figure in a velvet coat whom she immediately recognised from an oil painting as William Constable. But she was startled when the figure spoke: 'I wished to see what had been done to my room', he said. Restoration work since that encounter has revealed a spiral staircase leading from the place where the ghost materialised to the hall below.

Kraster and Dorothy Cook—Calgarth Hall, Windermere, Cumbria

A grisly haunting this, by two human skulls. They are those of the Cooks, husband and wife, who farmed on the banks of Windermere, neighbours of Squire Phillipson of Calgarth Manor. He coveted the Cooks' land and falsely accused them of stealing, and then, as local magistrate, sentenced them both to death. From the dock, Dorothy Cook cursed the Phillipson family to ruin, promising to haunt Calgarth for as long as the walls stand. Within months of the Cooks' execution, their skulls appeared at Calgarth, heralded by blood-curdling screams. For years they plagued the old house until the Phillipson family sank into poverty and obscurity.

Mary Anne Cotton—West Auckland, County Durham

Mary Cotton was tried at Durham Assizes in March 1873, for murder. She was charged with poisoning her fourth husband and four children and suspected of poisoning fifteen more people. *The Illustrated Police News* of the day described her as one of the most callous, wholesale murderers of the century. After her execution, and even in recent years, there were reports of her ghost, and those of some of her victims, haunting the churchyard in West Auckland where their bodies had been exhumed for dissection.

Bishop Coverdale—Church of St Magnus the Martyr, London

The figure which haunts St Magnus, described as 'a short, black-haired priest wearing a cassock with a cowl', may be Myles Coverdale, sixteenth-century Bishop of Exeter and, for a time rector, of this City church. Bishop Coverdale, first to translate the Bible into English, is buried here and the spectral brother was once seen bending over the Bishop's tomb. At other times it was observed kneeling before the Blessed Sacrament in the Lady Chapel.

Crier of Claife—Windermere, Cumbria

This is the name given to the ghost which, for years, haunted in the vicinity of Nab Ferry, on the shores of Lake Windermere. There are some who say that Crier Quarry and Crier Woods, near to High Wray, are still haunted. The legend dates from the fifteenth century when, one wild night, a cry for a ferry was heard from the Nab. The boatman who rowed out into the storm to answer the call returned alone and numb with horror. By morning he was mumbling deliriously and within a few days he was dead, without giving any clue as to what terrible experience he had been through, although for weeks after there were weird cries from across the water whenever the lake was lashed by storms. No boatman would row the ferry after dark, none of the local foxhounds would venture near to Crier Woods, and it is still a mystery what happened to the schoolmaster from Colthouse, who left his home to pass the Crier, but was never seen again.

Kit Crewbucket—Harecastle Tunnel, Staffordshire

'Too terrible to describe', say the old bargees, of Kit Crewbucket's ghost, that of a headless woman, thought to have been murdered, and dumped in the $2\frac{1}{4}$ mile long Harecastle Tunnel on the Trent and Mersey Canal. Narrow-boat folk of last century would navigate miles round to avoid the eeriness of the tunnel stretching under Golden Hill, at one end of which is Kidsgrove, from which the ghost derived its name, a corruption of Kidsgrove Boggart. Similarly, regular boatmen on the Shropshire Canal would go to great lengths to avoid tying up for the night in Betton Woods, near Market Drayton, because of a shrieking ghost.

Tom Crocker—Burgh Island, Devon

Tom Crocker was a pirate and smuggler, undisputed king of Burgh Island in the days when it was 10 acres of storm-lashed rock where he could pursue his illicit trade unmolested. Until recently, Crocker's pirate flag, grey and crumbling, had pride of place in the island's Pilchard Inn, and, according to all reports, his ghost still haunts there. He is particularly active in August, the anniversary of his hanging in 1395.

Oliver Cromwell—Apsley House, London W1

In earlier days, when the first Duke of Wellington lived at Apsley House, he encountered a ghostly figure, wearing plate armour, whom he recognised as Cromwell. It was in the winter of 1832, when England was on the brink of revolt over the Reform Bill and seething crowds besieged the Duke in his home. As the figure of the Lord Protector faced Wellington, he pointed meaningfully towards the angry mob. It was long after the bill was passed that the Duke revealed his ghostly experience which made him change his attitude about reform. Cromwell's ghost is seen to walk also in London's Red Lion Square, with John Bradshaw and General Ireton as spectral companions. After the restoration, the bodies of all three Parliamentarians were supposedly exhumed and taken by cart to Red Lion fields, then to Tyburn.

It is generally accepted that Cromwell and his top brass used the Golden Lion at St Ives, Huntingdon, as a regional HQ of the Parliamentary army. A shadowy shape of a man dressed in Cromwellian clothes seen in Room 13 is thought to be that of the Lord Protector, while the ghost of a woman, known as the Lady in Green, is reputed to have been Cromwell's mistress.

Squire Cunliffe—Wycoller Hall, near Colne, Lancashire

Once a year the ghost of Simon Cunliffe, swaggering Squire of Wycoller, comes back to the ruin of the old hall. This is where, in Stuart times, he thrashed his young wife to death for continually spurning his advances, and where, on the anniversary of the crime, his ghost re-enacts the whole harrowing scene, complete with agonised screams and dying groans. Then, as quickly as he came, he leaps into the saddle of his waiting horse, clatters over the narrow stone bridge, and gallops towards the moors.

The Cyclist—Stoneleigh Bridge, near Coventry, Warwickshire

In his Victorian youth, Thomas Eales, one of the last of Coventry's blacksmiths, was interested in bicycles. With his knickerbockered friends, he used to hurtle down the steep hill at Stoneleigh Bridge, each showing off their skill in taking the right-angled bend at the bottom. Until the day one of them crashed headlong into the wall and broke his neck. Though that accident happened in the 1880s, it has been witnessed since again and again—a ghostly 'playback' of the whole grim scene. A dramatic report from two women motoring down the Stoneleigh Bridge gradient, describes their alarm at seeing this 'old-fashioned cyclist on an old-fashioned bike' riding furiously in front of them, looking back and grimacing. They were sick with horror as he smashed into the stonework of the bridge, and speechless when, on running over to help, they found nothing.

D

Young Lord Dacre of Hurstmonceaux, Sussex

The ghosts of Lord Dacre and a gamekeeper have been seen at Hurstmonceaux since the sixteenth century. It is believed they stem from an encounter the young Lord, and three devil-may-care companions, had with a neighbour's gamekeepers, while out on a midnight poaching spree. What started as a lark ended in death for one of the keepers, felled by a blow from Lord Dacre's sword. While his young lordship's ghost rides in the castle grounds on a chestnut mare, the keeper has been seen in the field where he was struck down.

A certain elderly Lord Dacre who became a hermit, also haunts the castle, beating a drum as he did long ago to keep hopeful admirers away from his young and lovely wife. Lonely and frustrated beyond endurance, she barred the door of her husband's room, leaving him to starve and his ghost to drum on to eternity.

Grace Darling—Farne Islands, Northumberland

Trinity House keepers on the Longstone Lighthouse reckon to live with the ghost of Grace Darling, who was born in this lighthouse on the Farne Islands, in 1815. It was in 1838 that the steamer *Forfarshire* was wrecked off Longstone in a raging storm, through which twenty-three-year-old Grace and her father rowed to rescue nine survivors. Four years after that heroic rescue, Grace died of consumption. In a 1976 Tyne Tees Television interview, two keepers described the ghost they had encountered, independently of each other, while working in the lighthouse. One, the principal keeper, spoke of a ghostly female shape he saw in the engine room, while the other (new to the job) talked of the ghost, thought to be Grace Darling, walking about in what appeared to be clogs.

Rachel Darrell—Littlecote Manor, Wiltshire

'Wicked' Will Darrell of Littlecote had many mistresses, among them his own sister, Rachel, who, it is suggested, was the masked woman who had his child on a November night in 1575. Immediately it was born Darrell flung it on the blazing fire, ignoring the midwife's pleas to let her adopt it. What's more he pushed it deeper into the embers, presumably to ensure no features were recognisable. The room where the child was done to death so horribly is haunted by the wraith of a grieving woman with a baby in her arms, which some say is not Darrell's sister, but another of his mistresses, Elizabeth Benham.

Will Darrell—Littlecote Park, Wiltshire

Wild Will Darrell flirted not only with the law, but with every willing woman who came his way. In Elizabethan days his riproaring reputation as a man who would stop at nothing stretched far beyond the boundaries of his home, Littlecote Park. Even murder was acceptable if it suited his ends, as it did the night a child was born to one of his mistresses (see Rachel Darrell). Although Darrell was eventually charged with child murder, he escaped hanging, though not a sudden and violent death. He was flung from his horse while hunting in Littlecote Park and broke his neck at a spot now called Darrell's Stile. There his ghost is seen leading a pack of phantom hounds, causing horses to shy.

David Davies—Dartmoor, Devon

David Davies spent fifty years in prison. He first went to jail in 1879 and died in 1929 in Dartmoor, where he had a job he loved—shepherd to the prison flock. He became so trusted that, at lambing time, he slept out on the moor with the expectant ewes. At the time of his release, he asked to be allowed to remain and, being told 'no', pleaded that his shepherd's job be kept for him. 'I'll be back', he said as he left Princetown. He was back two weeks later and, according to some behind those grim granite walls, he's still to be seen on the moor at lambing time, tending the sheep from HM Prison.

John Dawson—Bashall Eaves, near Clitheroe, Lancashire

It was generally accepted that Farmer Dawson was a bachelor without an enemy in the world. Yet in March 1934 he was murdered, shot with a home-made steel bullet, as he returned home from the local one Sunday evening. Oddly, he did not know he'd been shot until the next morning, when he asked his sister to look at his back because it was hurting. Three days later he died, leaving behind one of the biggest murder mysteries ever, and a ghost which searches for something in the hedge, near the gate where he was shot.

Lady Dering—Pluckley, Kent

The Dering family squired Pluckley for 300 years from their manor of Surrenden Dering. Though now largely a fire-blackened ruin, the disastrous blaze of 1952 seemingly did not destroy the ghost of the White Lady, a former Lady Dering, said to be so beautiful that her husband had her embalmed to preserve her loveliness. Pluckley's Red Lady, another of the Dering girls, haunts the parish church. She is a sorrowing wraith seen near the family tomb and thought to be searching for the baby she lost.

This Wealden village, though not the most haunted in all England (see Bramshott, Hampshire), is certainly the most haunted in Kent, with a dozen ghosts ahaunting. The old watercress woman is by far the most interesting of these unnamed spectres. She was a local gypsy who dozed off to sleep while smoking her pipe, at the side of the Pinnock Stream, where she had been gathering cress. The gin-stained shawl about her bent shoulders caught fire and she burned to a gruesome death.

Lady Anna Derwentwater—Dilston Castle, Northumberland

Lady Anna was married at nineteen to the 3rd Earl of Derwentwater whose Jacobite sympathies led him to the battlefield at Preston and, finally, to the scaffold on Tower Hill, in 1716. The people of Dilston were shocked and angry at his death, blaming Lady Anna for encouraging him to join the ill fated rebellion. She was forced to leave the castle, moving from place to place to escape local indignation. Eventually, worn out with the constant upheavals and bitterness, she died by the time she was thirty. Her ghost has returned to the place she knew happiness—the now ruined Dilston Castle—watching for the homecoming of the young Earl, much as she did in the days before the uprising.

Doctor Dick—Conway, North Wales

Young Doctor Dick shares the haunting of Conway's Plas Mawr (Great Hall) with Sir Robert Wynne, the man who built the house in 1577. The doctor could not have been blamed for Lady Dorothy Wynne dying in childbirth, or for the death of her prematurely born infant. Neither, for that matter, was he responsible for her three-year-old's death after falling down stairs. But, locked by the housekeeper in the Lantern Room with the still-warm corpses, he panicked on hearing Sir Robert return to the house, and groped his way up the great chimney into the black unknown. Soon he was lost and overcome with smoke and fumes.

His bones have yet to be found in the labyrinth of chimney passages and attic hiding places, which, for four centuries, have housed his ghost.

Sir Robert Wynne, says the Plas Mawr legend, haunts the Lantern Room where he broke in to find the bodies of his wife and children. Spurning all words of reason and comfort, he yelled for vengeance on Dr Dick, swearing he would never leave that room until he'd found him—which he never has. In fact, after hours, if not days, of pacing and grieving, he collapsed in an exhausted state and died at the foot of the bed on which his dead wife lay.

Charles Dickens—Doughty Street, London

There are those who think the ghost of a short, but slim, figure in dark clothes and top hat, seen in the Doughty Street area, is Charles Dickens, who lived at No 48 for three years. Dickens himself certainly believed in the paranormal and published other people's psychic experiences in his journal *All The Year Round*. He also had some near-paranormal experiences of his own, as well as experimenting in psychic activities.

There have been accounts of a ghost, grey-bearded and top-hatted, with features resembling those of Dickens, walking in the old burial ground of Rochester Castle. His wish to be buried there was ignored.

Sir Everard Digby—North Luffenham Hall, Leicestershire

Sir Everard was a conspirator in the Gunpowder Plot. It was his job to prepare the Midlands for the general uprising, triggered by Guy Fawkes' blowing up of Parliament. North Luffenham would have been the centre of operations had not the whole mad, murderous scheme failed, resulting in arrest for Digby, and execution on 30 January 1606. Many people claim to have seen his ghost at the Hall, including the sister of one post-war owner who swears she was pinched by the spectre conspirator. Sir Everard is reputed to walk, as well, at Tilton Manor House, Leicestershire.

Dorothy Dingle—South Petherwin, Cornwall

Parson John Ruddle of Launceston left a detailed account of Dorothy Dingle's ghost which has haunted in the vicinity of Botathan's Farm since the 1660s. His attempts at exorcism were not successful in removing the wraith, which first appeared to the younger son of the Bligh's who, in those days, farmed hereabouts. Dorothy Dingle, who used to visit the family, was suspected of having died giving birth to a child supposedly fathered by the elder of the two Bligh boys.

Benjamin Disraeli—Hughenden Manor, Buckinghamshire

Disraeli, one of Queen Victoria's favourite prime ministers, lived most of his political life at Hughenden Manor, which he bought after marrying Wyndham Lewis's widow in 1839. His ghost walks the upper floors of this great house and was once seen with papers in its hand at the bottom of the stairs leading from the cellar. The study is exactly as it was when Disraeli died in 1881, by which time he had been raised to the peerage as Lord Beaconsfield.

Edward Dobsod—Market Street, Ludlow, Shropshire

Dobsod was a soldier of Tudor England on duty at Ludlow, where he died in a pub brawl in 1553. His ghost, a bewigged figure with a cloak around the shoulders, haunts The Globe, where he was murdered, in Market Street, the oldest part of the town and within a hundred yards of the now-ruined castle at which Dobsod was quartered.

In Ludlow's parish churchyard, the phantom of a tall elderly woman with grey hair, shuffles among the tombstones, dressed in a long, drab-coloured robe. She is seen also near the rectory.

Lady Dodington—Breamore House, Hampshire

For more than two centuries, ten generations of the Hulse family have owned Breamore and shared their home with a ghost of the Dodingtons who built this Elizabethan mansion in 1585.

This spectre is a Grey Lady wearing a poke bonnet, reputed to be the wife of Sir William Dodington. She was murdered in 1629 by her son, Henry, who was hanged for the crime at Winchester, the following year. Legend says she makes only rare appearances—on the impending death of an owner of Breamore.

William Doggett—Eastbury House, Dorset

Doggett was steward to Earl Temple who lived at Eastbury in the 1790s. He swindled his lordship in so many ways that when he was eventually found out he shot himself. Blood stains are still on the floor at Eastbury to prove it, while his ghost haunts not only the house, but also the long yew-shaded drive. There, a headless coachman with a headless four-in-hand has been seen to stop to pick up Doggett's ghost, which is easily identified by the yellow ribbons with which he tied his knee breeches. In 1845, his coffin was exhumed, to reveal a rosy-faced corpse with no signs of decay, which caused the villagers of Tarrant Gunville to think Doggett was a vampire.

Father Dominique—The Crown Inn, Pishill, Oxford

There is a stone in Pishill churchyard marking the grave of Father Dominique, whose ghost walks at The Crown, a figure in a black cloak and wide-brimmed hat. He met his death fighting to protect a girl he had fallen in love with, against the obscenities of a young buck who wouldn't take no for an answer. Impulsively Father Dominique came out of hiding, seized a sword from the wall and challenged the man to a duel. Within minutes his inexpert swordmanship allowed him to be struck down, mortally wounded.

Nurse Dowdall—Burton Constable Hall, near Hull, Humberside

The shade of Nurse Dowdall, a nineteenth-century nanny so much revered by the Constable family that when she died she was laid to rest in the family mausoleum, has stayed on in the old home she knew and loved practically all her life. Nanny's ghost lingers in Stephen's Tower, seen by all but one of the women in the family.

Oldest of the Hall's spectral residents is a nun, sighted in the Long Gallery, and seen to disappear at the door of what is known as the Nun's Room.

Outside, in the 750-acre park which encompasses the Hall, is a whole army of ghosts, phantom figures of Roman soldiers which haunt the tree-fringed drive leading to the east front of the house.

Sir Francis Drake—Dartmoor, Devon

Dartmoor is so alive with legends about Drake and his ghost that it's hard to sort the fact from the fiction. Although Buckland Abbey was his home, he does not seem to haunt there, but out on the moor, along the old road, between Plymouth and Tavistock. He is seen riding with a pack of spectral hounds, or, at other times, driving a black hearse-like coach, pulled by four headless black horses, with headless hounds running beside the lurching vehicle. Even Nutwell Court, near Exton, where the Drake family lived after Sir Francis died in 1596, is reputed to have his ghost. On the road that passes the house is seen the ghost of Eliott Drake, haunting the spot where he fell from his horse and broke his neck.

William Drury—Tidworth, Wiltshire

This was a well documented seventeenth-century case of poltergeist manifestation, investigated on behalf of Charles II by a Royal Commission. Drury eventually admitted to being 'The Demon Drummer' and was sentenced to be transported for witchcraft. His ghost returned and the drumming went on, in fact it can still be heard, according to some who travel that road to Salisbury.

It is not to be confused with the drummer-boy of Salisbury Plain, murdered for his pay by a colour-sergeant, in the 1770s. Some years after, the sergeant, walking at the murder spot, saw the boy's ghost and heard his ghostly drumming. He broke down and confessed, and was subsequently hanged.

Charlotte Dymond—Bodmin Moor, Cornwall

A stone memorial to Charlotte Dymond marks the place on Bodmin Moor where this eighteen-year-old farm-girl from Penhale died on a spring Sunday afternoon in 1844. Matt Weeks, her lame boyfriend, maddened by her talk of going with other men, put an end to her tormenting by cutting her throat on the little-trodden path that skirted Roughtor. To this day Charlotte is said to haunt the slopes of this second highest tor in Cornwall, walking nightly in this still-wild, desolate place, in her gown of many colours, red shawl and silk bonnet.

Another of the moor's ghosts is that which lingers in the vicinity of Jamaica Inn, the shade of a seaman murdered for his shore-pay while making his way from Plymouth to Penzance.

E

Sir Robert Earnley—Sidlesham, Sussex

Sir Robert was a Royalist, one of King Charles's men defending Chichester. On the day of the city's eventual surrender to Cromwell's forces, Sir Robert, with a Cavalier escort, galloped to Sidlesham, hopeful of escaping to France with his two nephews. But, before they could board ship, they were ambushed by pursuing Parliamentary troops, on the quay opposite the Crab and Lobster Inn. Sir Robert died along with his four companions, fighting to the end and there his ghost walks, a tall uniformed figure, a cloak about his shoulders, seen usually in the small hours.

Lady Editha—Tamworth Castle, Staffordshire

Alfred the Great's grand-daughter, Editha, is one of the ghosts that haunts Tamworth, as a Black Lady, because of the nun's habit in which she is seen on the stairs leading to the Tower Room. Her sighs and moans coming from the tower have been tape recorded. Editha founded the nunnery in the old Saxon castle which, after the battle of Hastings, was given to Robert de Marmion, for his support of the Conqueror. Robert immediately evicted the nuns, causing the irate ghost of Editha to appear and reproach him for his cruelty. Legend has it she hit him with her crosier, causing bleeding which only stopped when he vowed to show the nuns more compassion.

Tamworth's other ghost is a White Lady who saw Sir Lancelot kill her lover, the Saxon knight Sir Tarquin. The Grey Lady, which haunts at Ladye Place in the Thames Valley, is thought to be Editha, believed to have been buried there in the ruined twelfth-century priory.

Edward, The Martyr—Shaftesbury, Dorset

Labouring up the well worn cobbles of Shaftesbury's picturesque Gold Hill, the ghosts of two men leading pack horses, have been seen. With them they carry the body of the murdered boy-king, Edward, stabbed in the back at Corfe in 979, by his stepmother, Queen Elfrida. It is said in old chronicles that miracles happened as the body was being taken to Shaftesbury, where the King became St Edward the Martyr, and was enshrined in the abbey on the hill top.

Within the abbey ruins, another ghost haunts—a Benedictine monk who hid the community's treasure shortly before the Dissolution, but died of a heart attack before he could show Abbess Souche its whereabouts.

Elaine—Haden Hill, Worcestershire

Legend has it that a miller's daughter, named Elaine, haunts the Park House at Haden Hill. She was said to be a serving girl in early Tudor times, with a lover who was a monk from Manor Abbey at Halesowen. Together they hid in the cellars of the Park House, planning to elope and marry. Instead they were trapped and left to starve to death. Nocturnal users of the park, now the grounds of a museum and public library, have reported seeing 'the ghost of a girl with golden hair' gliding down the steps from the house. Museum staff are constantly hearing inexplicable footsteps and trying to account for lights being switched on after closing time.

Queen Elizabeth—Windsor Castle, Berkshire

Elizabeth reigned for forty-five glorious years and died, unmarried, at Richmond's long-ago demolished Royal Palace. She was psychic and, shortly before her death, had a vision in which she saw herself on her death bed 'pallid, shrivelled and wan'. For her ghost one has to go to Windsor where Lieutenant Carr Glynn of the Grenadiers, reading in the castle library (formerly the State apartments), heard footsteps and looked up to see the tall, stately figure of Queen Bess coming towards him. Emperor Frederick of Prussia had a similar experience.

A spectral royal coach, carrying the ghostly Elizabeth north from Greenwich to her hunting lodge in Epping Forest, is a psychic experience occasionally reported from Wanstead Park. Seemingly she went there not so much for the sport, but to meet discreetly with one of her favourites, Dudley, Earl of Leicester.

King Ella—Horning, Norfolk

According to legend, every five years on 21 July, Ella is recrowned King of East Anglia over which he ruled after the Roman withdrawal in AD 410. This ghostly coronation conducted by the Lord Abbot of Norwich, is re-enacted at Horning beside the River Bure, downstream from the Swan Inn, named after Ella, the Swan of Peace.

A mile further along the river, at the Old Ferry Inn, there is another spectral flashback, every twenty years. It is a September ghost of a young local girl who was seized by drunken monks working in the brewhouse, raped and disposed of in the river.

The Evangelist—Chichester Harbour, Hampshire

The ghost of a one-legged man, seen in the vicinity of Langstone Harbour, is remembered as an old evangelist who hobbled around on a crutch, carrying a haversack from which he handed out miniature bibles and scripture cards. He was thin and tall, with very little hair and a Duke of Wellington nose. Those who have encountered this ghost say the figure was lying on the ground stark naked, and vanished when they got within a few yards of it. Seemingly this one-legged preacher died on the edge of the creek which forms the harbour, perhaps after being attacked and robbed in the quiet, shady lane leading down to the mud flats.

There is no connection between this ghost and that which haunts the nearby Royal Oak—the shade of a woman, seen once to glide across a bedroom and vanish into a full-length mirror.

F

Faith—The Blue Ball, Soyland, West Yorkshire

Faith worked at this moorland pub in the eighteenth century, when it was notorious as a meeting place for thieves, gamblers and highwaymen. The landlord known for miles around as Iron Ned, was notorious too—as a ruthless seducer of women. With Faith he did not stop at seduction; he drowned her on the moors when he ultimately grew tired of her. Said Major Denis Siddall, late landlord of the Blue Ball: 'On quiet winters' nights, you can hear Faith's ghost run across the floor of Iron Ned's bedroom, desperately trying to escape his lecherous clutches'.

Guy Fawkes—Scotton Old Hall, Nidderdale, north Yorkshire

It is the ghost of young Guy which haunts the lanes and footpaths of Nidderdale, and sometimes the corridors of the Old Hall. He was only eight when his father died, so he spent most of his teens with his mother and stepfather at Percy House, Scotton, doing much as he pleased, walking, sometimes riding, often as far as Ripley Castle, to visit the Ingilbys. Guido Fawkes, the notorious gunpowder plotter does not seem to have left behind a conpisratorial ghost, only a happy, though aimless, one in adolescence.

Lady Katherine Ferrers—Markyate, Hertfordshire

Lady Kate was married at thirteen. By twenty-one she was bored with her marriage and looking for excitement. Dressed as a man, she took to robbing travellers on Watling Street, dropping on her unsuspecting victims from trees overhanging the road. Those clever tactics failed only once—the night she was fatally shot by the guard on a coach she waylaid near Markyate. Not only is her ghost still marauding the A5 on moonless nights, to remind us of the wicked lady she was, but both film maker and brewer have perpetuated her memory on celluloid and pub-sign.

There is another ghost which frequents the A5, between Dunstable and Markyate, that of a cricketer, killed in a road accident while returning from a match near Woburn Abbey, in 1958.

Finny—Crafthole, Cornwall

Finny was the name of a freetrader who headed a smuggling gang operating off the beaches of Whitsand Bay. Their headquarters was the New Inn on the Torpoint to Looe coast road, where Finny was surprised by the revenue men and killed in the resulting skirmish. He left behind a ghost, which, in 1950, caused the brewers to give the old pub a new name—The Finnygook—in his honour.

Mary Fitton—Gawsworth, Cheshire

The permissive Mary Fitton who, at seventeen, joined the Court of Queen Elizabeth I, is said to haunt at Gawsworth Old Hall. More accurately, her ghost is reputed to walk in the evening through the long avenue of lime trees leading to the Hall from the Macclesfield to Congleton road. It is a walk she must have done many times in her early carefree teens, before swopping the simple pleasures of Gawsworth for the temptations of Her Majesty's Court.

Sir Reginald Fitz Urse—Featherstone Castle, Northumberland

Sir Reginald died a horrible death in the great tower of Featherstone, where he was imprisoned and left to starve and where his groaning ghost has been heard re-enacting the dying knight's last agonised hours.

Another spectral resident seen within the castle is a Green Lady, who walks the ancient corridors in a gown of greenish-brown.

Sarah Fletcher—Clifton Hampden, Oxford

'... a martyr to excessive sensibility', says the tombstone epitaph to Sarah Fletcher, a beautiful innocent of twenty-nine who hanged herself from the curtain rail of her four-poster bed when she discovered her naval officer husband planned to bigamously marry another. Since that June day in 1799, when she did the deed with her pocket handkerchief and a piece of cord, her ghost has roamed the Georgian house in Clifton Hampden, a wraith with a purple ribbon in her curled, auburn hair, a long black silk cloak around her shoulders and a look of anguish in her eyes.

Dorothy Forster—Lord Crewe Arms, Blanchland, Northumberland

Dorothy Forster's claim to fame was engineering the spectacular escape of her brother, Thomas, from London's Newgate Prison. Held there for helping to plot the Jacobite rebellion in 1715, he was surely destined for the scaffold, unless sprung and smuggled to France. Dorothy ingeniously did all of that before returning to the Forster family home at Blanchland, once a monastery and now the Lord Crewe Arms. Dorothy's ghost is said to haunt the premises, seemingly looking for her exiled brother.

Jonas Fosbrooke—Ware, Hertfordshire

Jonas was the carpenter who made the 12ft square Great Bed of Ware, now in the Victoria and Albert Museum, in South Kensington. When it previously occupied most of one room at an inn at Ware, Hertfordshire, those who slept in it claimed they were pinched, beaten and scratched and the ghost of Fosbrooke was blamed. He intended the bed for Henry VIII and, because the

King never deigned to use it, has shown his annoyance by making it uncomfortable for others to sleep in.

Freddie Fredericks—Theatre Royal, Stratford East, London

The man who built the Theatre Royal in 1880 still keeps a spectral eye on it. According to some, he appears at least once nightly to check that the initials of his name, Freddie Fredericks, remain visible in the centre of the arch spanning the stage. Superstition has it that when they are removed, or painted over, the final curtain will come down for good. The late Gerry Raffles, who managed the theatre for more than twenty years, described the ghost as 'a small, tubby fellow, dressed in brown . . . of whom there's no need to be afraid'.

Reverend Maurice Frost—Debbington, Oxfordshire

For close on forty years, Maurice Frost was the Vicar of Debbington. After his death in 1962, his ghost returned to his old home, seemingly to keep a spectral eye on his most cherished books and to wind the collection of antique clocks.

Edwin Fry—The Blueberry Inn, Blewbury, Berkshire

Edwin Fry was landlord of this pub when it was called The New Inn. His regulars knew him then as 'Old Edwin' and today know his ghost by the same affectionate name. It walks from the upstairs bedroom, which used to be his until his death in 1951, to the bar downstairs. The footsteps are described as 'hollow and rubbery', the sound made by somebody walking in wellington boots.

The Fugitive—Marlpit's Hill, Devon

An unknown soldier of the battle of Sedgemoor haunts south of Honiton on Marlpit's Hill. It is a ghost that has been seen several times, once by a party of school-children, who watched the dazed-looking man in a black, broad-brimmed hat and long brown coat coming towards them, while their teacher saw nothing. The thatched cottage, now demolished, by which the children saw the ghost, was once the home of this fugitive from Monmouth's ill fated rebellion. As he staggered towards his front door, Royal troopers rode over the hill and butchered him in front of his wife and children.

G

Farmer Gammon—Exmoor, Devon-Somerset border

The melancholy figure of Farmer Gammon haunts the desolation that is called The Chains, the bogland between Exe Head and Pinkworthy Pond. As a widower from Bowley Barton, he was already an unhappy man, driven to desperation because the woman he wanted to make his second wife turned him down. He set out one day in 1889, stumbling hopelessly through Yarbury Coombe to the manmade tarn at Pinkworthy where he drowned himself in its black depths.

Jimmy Garlickhythe—Garlick Hill, London

Because nobody is able to put an acceptable identity to the mummified corpse found during nineteenth-century excavations at St James's Church, Garlick Hill, it has been dubbed Old Jimmy Garlickhythe. Possible identities? One of six early City lord mayors, their tombs being destroyed in the Great Fire, or Richard Rothing, who built the first church in 1326. The mummy is at least 500 years old and in a remarkable state of preservation in its glass-fronted coffin which had a narrow escape in the 1942 blitz. That presumably activated Jimmy's ghost—'a dried-up corpse'—seen since in the nave and at the top of the stairs leading to the balcony.

Kitty Garthwaite—Gillamoor, North Yorkshire

Kitty Garthwaite, lived, loved and died on the north Yorkshire moors. She was a Gillamoor girl, courting Willie Dixon, a boy from neighbouring Hutton le Hole. When he heard she was expecting his child, he deserted her and, on Whit Sunday evening in 1787, she drowned herself in the river Dove. Four days later, Willie also was found dead at the same place, after which villagers reported seeing Kitty's ghost sitting 'stark nakt' under the tree where she and Willie used to meet. But it was always men who saw her, sixteen of whom were lured by her charms to a watery grave, before the Vicar of Listingham finally exorcised 'Sarkless Kitty', as her naked ghost is called.

Sir John Gates—Beeleigh Abbey, Essex

Sir John lost his head on Tower Hill for supporting Lady Jane Grey. During the brief kingship of Edward VI, he had been captain of the Royal guard and, before that, a firm favourite of Henry VIII who let him buy Beeleigh for £300. There his ghost still walks, usually on the anniversary of his execution in 1553. He walks in the James Bedroom in the orthodox head-under-arm style.

Piers Gaveston—Scarborough Castle, North Yorkshire

Who is the silent shadowy figure legend has it lurks in the ruins of Scarborough's castle? A Gascon immigrant, called Piers Gaveston, Earl of Cornwall and gay young friend of King Edward II of England. It was at Scarborough that Gaveston surrendered to the barons, on condition his life be spared to stand trial. But he never did, as he was abducted on the journey south and beheaded at Warwick as a public enemy. His ghost seemingly seeks vengeance for being cheated of justice, lunging at anybody brave enough to walk among the ruins after dark.

George II—Kensington Palace, London

George II and his consort Caroline of Auspach used Kensington Palace as their home until the King's death in the autumn of 1760. He was on the English throne for more than thirty years, but never grew fond of the country. Daily he showed his preference for his native Hanover, by gazing from the palace windows towards the weathervane above the main entrance, watching for a favourable wind that would hasten the ships bringing despatches from Germany. Since his death, his ashen-faced ghost has been seen doing the same thing, his lips moving as if muttering 'Vy tont dey com?', as he did two centuries before.

King George III—Windsor Castle, Berkshire

George III became permanently insane in 1810 and, on his eldest son being made Regent the following year, the old King was confined to Windsor Castle, where he lived until he died in 1820, aged eighty. Most of his time in confinement, he spent playing the harp. His ghost walks in the rooms below the castle library, where he spent the last years of his life. Sentries on guard outside, looking up on hearing a tapping at the window, have seen the bearded old man staring out at them with wide, insane eyes.

George IV (The Prince Regent)—Brighton, Sussex

Where else would George IV haunt but Brighton? Where else but at the place he loved the most, that fabulous Indian-style Pavilion in which he, as Prince Regent, and Mrs Fitzherbert lived after their secret marriage? In its Regency heyday, two underground passages linked the Pavilion with the stables, now the Dome, and it is along those passages the Prince's spectre is seen walking. Years ago it was encountered also in the tunnel which ran from the cellars of the Druid's Head to the royal cellars, the route by which he is said to have received his supplies of smuggled liquor.

The Ghost Train—Box Tunnel, Wiltshire

The ghost train of Box Tunnel was no figment of the imagination to permanent waymen of the old Great Western Railway. Many of them working in the 1¾ mile long tunnel, in the later days of steam, were convinced of either seeing or hearing the phantom express roar by. In the first few years after Brunel's 'masterpiece, was opened in 1841, many travellers were afraid of going through' not because of any ghost train, but for fear of suffocation. Others, knowing it was 300ft below surface in places, feared it might collapse, so left the train to go by road to the far end of the tunnel.

Sir Walter Giffard—Weare Giffard, Devon

Sir Walter lived at the manor of Weare Giffard, near Great Torrington, until his death in 1267. Since then his ghost is said to walk at midnight in search of the wife he left behind. It is on record in the village church that the phantom knight has been seen gliding from the gatehouse of the old manor, along the road to the churchyard. Using the ancient knocker he raps on the south door which creaks open, and Sir Walter disappears inside.

Tobias Gill—Blythburgh, Suffolk

Black Toby, as he was otherwise known, was a negro drummer in the 4th Hussars. In June 1750, having got drunk in the White Hart at Blythburgh, he raped and throttled Ann Blakemore, a pretty young girl who was walking home to Walberswick. Three farm hands found them at dawn lying together on the heath, the girl dead, Black Toby still in a drunken sleep. He was sentenced at Bury St Edmunds and gibbeted on Blythburgh Heath, where not a soul would walk at night for years afterwards, for fear of a ghostly presence which is said to persist even today.

Gilsland Boy—Triermain Castle, Gilsland, Northumberland

The Gilsland Boy is the ghost of a child, a frightened, snivelling six year old with a thin, reedy voice sobbing the words 'Cauld for ever mair' through chattering teeth. This harrowing spectre stems from about the mid-fifteenth century when Triermain was a flourishing fort, left to an orphaned boy with an evil uncle as his ward. To get his hands on the child's inheritance the uncle starved his nephew until he was almost too weak to stand, then left him on nearby Thirwell Common in a raging snowstorm. To see his ghost is said to portend trouble, though usually it is the touch of tiny icy fingers on yours that makes one aware of his presence.

Henry Girdlestone—Abbey Hostel Hotel, Crowland, Lincolnshire

Had there been a *Guinness Book of Records* in 1844, farmer Henry Girdlestone's name would have been in it for his astonishing feat of walking more than a thousand miles in a thousand consecutive hours. Never one to refuse a wager, he started from the Abbey Hostel hotel in East Street, Crowland, on the morning of 1 February, walked in a gigantic circle around the Lincolnshire countryside, finishing forty-nine days later, back at Crowland. He then slept for three days and went on to live to a ripe old age, leaving a ghost that goes on walking in the attic of the Abbey, though, at times, a little wearily.

Judge John Glanville—Tavistock, Devon

The conscience-stricken ghost of Judge John has walked Kilworthy House for centuries, ever repentant for sentencing his own daughter to death. She, Elizabeth Glanville, is said also to haunt this much-restored sixteenth-century mansion, having been seen in one of the bedrooms and heard on the stairs—which is remarkable since she never lived here, but at the old Glanville home at Halwell. It was there that tragedy overtook her young life. Elizabeth was in love with a naval lieutenant, which displeased the Judge who forced her to marry someone he considered more suitable—a Plymouth goldsmith named Page. Helped by her maid and her sailor lover, Elizabeth murdered the goldsmith and, within days, all three were arrested and put on trial before her father, who subsequently ordered her and her accomplices to be hanged.

Robert Glover—Mancetter Manor, Warwickshire

Robert Glover, one of three brothers, was a staunch Protestant at a time when that religion was a dirty word. Early in the sixteenth century, the family bought Mancetter Manor with its warren of secret passages, living there quietly until 1555. Then life was shattered by a warning that Mary Tudor's men had orders to arrest them. Had Robert not been ill he would have escaped with his brothers; as it was he was dragged from his sick bed to face trial as a heretic and death at the stake. His ghost is said to walk in the bedroom that was his, known today as the Martyr's Room.

Nearby Atherstone is haunted by a farmer who had a wager on the time it would take to ride by night from Atherstone to Alderminster. In his haste he was knocked from the saddle by an overhanging tree and killed, leaving his ghost to complete the ride.

Police Sergeant Goddard—Vine Street Police Station, London

Sergeant Goddard was a station sergeant at Vine Street early this century. He committed suicide by hanging himself in one of the cells, leaving behind a ghost which stayed on duty, even when the Metropolitan Police vacated the premises during World War II. Since the police reoccupied Vine Street, Sergeant Goddard has gone on pounding the corridors, opening locked cell doors and disturbing documents.

Edward Golding—Ilmington, Warwickshire

Until his death, in 1793, Edward Golding was the parish clerk of Ilmington. Not long after he'd been buried, in the shadow of the village church that had been so much part of his life, his ghost came back to haunt it. He was seen—though not of late—walking to and fro in the nave, muttering the responses, as he had done every Sunday since a lad in the choir.

Ilmington's night coach (seen also in daylight), was first reported in 1780 by a farmer walking home along Pig Lane one foggy night. He was so preoccupied with his thoughts, he barely noticed the stage-coach pulled by six phantom horses silently pass him by. It was going like the wind towards the hills above the village, and not until it was lost in the mist, did he realise he had not heard its approach. Then something also occurred to him: the coach and team was not travelling on a hard road but over a rough track where no ordinary coach could possibly go at such speed.

Margaret Gould (Old Madam)—Lewtrenchard, Devon

'Old Madam' was the name by which Mrs Margaret Gould was known locally in Lewtrenchard. She was the grandmother of the Reverend Sabine Baring-Gould, author of 150 books and of that rousing hymn, *Onward Christian Soldiers*. He died in 1924. She died on 10 April 1795, sitting in her high-backed chair because she refused to go to bed. Within an hour of her death her ghost was seen in the garden and has since been seen very many times by very many people; she has a particular attachment for the Long Gallery.

Charlie Gordon—Albion Inn, Bill Quay, Felling, Tyne and Wear

A tall man in a grey suit and a black Homburg hat; that's old Charlie Gordon as the regulars at the Albion knew him. And that's how they now see his ghost, standing near the serving hatch, or sitting at the bar, much as he did practically every day of his life. For sixty years, since a lad in his teens, he'd been calling in at this pub and when he died after World War II, the whole neighbourhood mourned the passing of the man they all knew as 'the Gentleman of Bill Quay'.

Lady Elizabeth Gray—The George Inn, Silsoe, Bedfordshire

Lady Elizabeth, headstrong daughter of a wealthy squire, has haunted The George since the time she hid at the inn to be near her coachman lover. She died when the coach in which they were eloping, pursued by her irate father, careered off the road into a lake.

The Grenadier—Wilton Row, London

This is one of London's best known ghosts: a young guards officer of the Duke of Wellington's regiment, who died after a thrashing for cheating at cards. That was in the early 1800s, when The Grenadier pub in Wilton Row was called less grandly The Guardsman, and part of it was the regimental mess where officers dined, wined and gambled. The unfortunate subaltern caught cheating faced a kangaroo court which sentenced him to a flogging, at the end of which he staggered to the top of the cellar stairs and fell headlong to his death. Presumably this happened in September, since that is when his ghost is seen both on the stairs and in a bedroom, by successive landlords and their families.

Sir Fulke Greville—Warwick Castle, Warwick

This Elizabethan poet, who became the 1st Lord Brooke, was stabbed while visiting London in 1628. An old and trusted servant, whom he took with him from Warwick Castle, turned on his master, then turned the knife on himself. Sir Fulke, who lingered for a month before dying, lingers still as a ghost in his old study where he did much of his writing. It remains furnished as it was in his time of occupation.

Lady Jane Grey—Tower of London

Lady Jane, Queen of England for just nine days, lost her head on Tower Green on 12 February 1554. She was only twenty-six and, before going to the block, witnessed a grim sight—the beheaded body of her husband, Lord Guildford Dudley, brought back from Tower Hill on a cart. Her ghost and that of her husband haunt the Tower, though not together. She, a gentle ghost, has been seen on the anniversary of her execution, 'a strange, white apparition' high on the battlements of the Salt Tower. A happier Lady Jane haunts the mansion which was briefly her childhood home at Kinver, Staffordshire, now the Whittington Inn.

Jo Grimaldi—Sadler's Wells Theatre, London

When only three years old, Jo Grimaldi began his stage career; he danced, in 1781, at Sadler's Wells, the theatre in which he was to make his name as the most famous of English clowns. It is not surprising that his ghost haunts The Wells, his long, white-painted face peering out from one of the boxes, two glassy eyes staring into the darkness of the auditorium. At Drury Lane, where Grimaldi first went on as a pantomime clown—and forty-five years later made his farewell appearance—his ghostly presence is also felt, though more as a comforting, guiding influence, by newcomers to this famous stage.

Lady Anne Grimston—Tewin Water, Hertfordshire

In her lifetime, Lady Anne is reputed to have denied the Resurrection and doubted the existence of God. It was no surprise, therefore, when, on her deathbed, she was heard to say 'If there is any truth in the word of God, may seven trees grow on my grave'. That was in 1716, since when a multi-trunked sycamore and several ash trees have grown through her tomb in the village churchyard, and her ghost is doomed to haunt the grounds of her former home, Tewin Water.

Lady Cathcart, who was married four times and hoped to make it five before she died aged ninety-seven, also haunts.

Hannah Grundy—Staithes, North Yorkshire

Hannah, a fishwife of the early 1800s, died a sudden and grisly death on the beach at Staithes. She was decapitated at the foot of Boulby Cliff, while bait gathering. A falling rock struck her on the neck and scythed off her head, leaving a headless wraith to mingle with today's holiday crowds.

The Guardsman—Windsor Castle, Berks

One of the best documented of the ghosts of Windsor; not a phantom Royal but a serving soldier who, in 1927, shot himself while on sentry duty in the Long Walk. Weeks later, another guardsman, an eighteen-year-old grenadier, was patrolling the Long Walk in the early hours of the morning, when he saw another sentry marching towards him. He thought at first it was his relief, until he recognised the face below the bearskin headdress as that of the soldier who shot himself while patrolling the same eerie beat. Back in the guardroom, he learned that the sentry he relieved also did duty with the ghost.

Martha Gunn—Brighton, Sussex

Martha Gunn was a celebrity at Brighton for three-quarters of a century. She was one of the Prince Regent's favourite 'dippers' (the other being Old Smoaker) who assisted bathers in taking their morning dip from the bathing machines. This 'Queen of the Dippers', as she was known, was often invited to Brighton's Royal Pavilion by the Prince, later George IV. Not only has his ghost been seen in the Pavilion, but also that of Martha Gunn, usually haunting in the kitchens.

'George' Gutsell—Parsonage Lane, Icklesham, Sussex

This ghost is no transparent figure, but portly and 'solid looking', in shirt sleeves, and a rough tweed waistcoat joined across the front by a heavy, gold watch chain. The local folk, old enough to be in the know, say he's a long-dead landlord of the Queen's Head, named Gutsell, who they fondly call 'George'. He sports a beard, side-whiskers and a moustache, and frequents the bar, usually sitting in a chair in front of the fire. When he died in 1890, close on seventy, he was laid out in his coffin on the bar-counter and given a rousing send-off by his customers.

Rosamund Guy—Irby, Humberside

Locally the ghost of Rosamund is known as the 'Irby Boggle', which makes its presence felt in various ways in the flatlands that stretch from Irby to the Humber estuary. It is a veteran among boggles, dating from a November evening in 1455, when Rosamund met Neville Randall, the man she was soon to wed, in Irby Dale copse and died by his hand after a lovers' tiff escalated into a violent quarrel.

Mistress Eleanor Gwynn—Salisbury Hall, Hertfordshire

'Witty, pretty Nellie', as a ghost, is as flamboyant as her seventeenth-century flesh-and-blood original. When seen at Salisbury Hall, favourite summer hideaway of herself and King Charles, the phantom Nell is in the blue fichu in which Lely painted her portrait. At London's Gargoyle night club, formerly her Soho house, she is a shadowy figure in high-waisted dress with a cartwheel hat and pungent gardenia perfume. At Charles's Northamptonshire retreat, Salcey Lawn, she has been seen doing nothing more exciting than sitting in the orchard, though it is there, supposedly, that bored Nell took another lover, whom the King had murdered. His ghost, too, wanders in adjoining woods.

H

The Hairy Hands—of Dartmoor, Devon

There are several cases on record of car drivers and motor cyclists who, while crossing Dartmoor, have had their steering wheels or handle bars wrenched from their control by a pair of large, muscular, hairy hands. The place at which these spectral hands—not usually visible—take over and force the driver to stop or have a serious accident is on the Two Bridges to Moretonhampstead road near Postbridge. It is no new phenomenon; in 1921 the medical officer for Dartmoor Prison was killed as a result of it, while it was a dreaded experience in the days of horse and coach traffic.

Lady Constance Hall—Bexley, Kent

It's difficult to imagine Bexley in the days when deer ran wild in this part of Kent and Sir Thomas Atte Hall was gored to death by a cornered stag in the courtyard of Hall Place which, in the thirteenth century, was his manor. The ghost, which has walked ever since, is not that of Sir Thomas, but of his distraught wife, Lady Constance, who threw herself off the tower after seeing her husband killed. For years, moans have been heard in the tower and the figure of a woman in white has repeatedly re-enacted the death fall.

John Hampden—Clifton Hampden, Oxfordshire

Hampden, cousin of Oliver Cromwell, was the politician largely responsible for the chain of events that led to the Civil War. When the fighting began, he took up arms against the King and was an early victim of Prince Rupert's cavalry. Since the family estate embraced the village of Clifton Hampden, The Plough was very much his local; there is a room named in his honour and his Puritan ghost treads its ancient boards.

King Harold—Battle Abbey, Sussex

It is a myth that Harold, last of the Saxon kings, died as a result of a Norman arrow shot into his eye at Sanlac Hill. Harold died on that October day in 1066 of a deep sword wound in his thigh, which is why reports of his ghost being seen at Battle Abbey, 'complete with an arrow in the head and dripping blood', are difficult to accept.

Other reported hauntings from the Abbey are a friar who walks near the Monk's Wall and a knight seen in the Great Hall, holding a long sword.

George Hastilow—Aston Cross Brewery, Birmingham

This is a ghost of pre-war vintage, thought to be George Hastilow, who drove a bottle wagon for Ansell's, the Midland brewers. He was always well turned-out in jacket and breeches, a cravat secured with a stock-pin, gaiters and boots polished until you could see your face in them. Which is how his ghost is seen today, haunting the site of the old brewery stables.

One of Ansell's pubs, The Manor House in West Bromwich has two ghosts, bequeathed from the days when it was The Old Hall—a man with a black beard and a grey-haired woman, believed to be an eighty-year-old grandmother, burnt to death after falling into the fire.

Sir Henry Hawkins—Middle Temple, London

Sir Henry, the 'hanging judge' who later became Lord Brampton, is thought to be the ghost which haunts the ancient precincts of the Temple. It is a bewigged figure, wearing a black gown with a bulging file of documents under one arm. It is little different to any one of the many other striding barristers hurrying towards the neighbouring Law Courts, except this figure is usually seen late at night, noiselessly *gliding* through the cloisters, or as daylight is fading and the Temple lamplighter is going his rounds, much as he did in Sir Henry's prime.

George Haydock—Mowbreck Hall, Wesham, Lancashire

In Victorian times, the Gory Head of Mowbreck was not a tale to be scoffed at. The mill folk of Kirkham and Wesham would not venture after dusk up the tree-shaded drive to the Hall, for fear of seeing a manifestation of the severed, bloodstained head of George Haydock, a young priest who was betrayed and executed in London in 1584. His father, seeing this horrific vision the night his son was arrested, died from shock. In recent years nothing more grisly has been reported than weird noises and mysterious footsteps tramping from the front door up the stairs to a priest's hide.

Maud Heath—Wick Hill, near Bremhill, Wiltshire

If Maud Heath wanted to get to Chippenham Market she went by way of flooded fields and rutted cart tracks, at times ankle deep in mud and water. There was no other way in fifteenth-century England, which is why this Wiltshire widow willed her life savings, when she died in 1474, for building four miles of dry even pathway from Wick Hill to Chippenham. Known to this day as Maud Heath's Causeway, it is reputed to be haunted by Maud's ghost, a figure in homespun and bonnet and carrying a basket, just as she is depicted on top of her monument, close to Bremhill.

King Henry VI—Muncaster Castle, Ravenglass, Cumbria

Henry's ghost has haunted Muncaster since the day he was done to death in the Tower of London, in 1471. When he was on the run during the Wars of the Roses, he was given safe refuge in the castle by Sir John Pennington, one of the few nobles who offered hospitality to the hunted King.

Muncaster has another ghost, the headless shade of a humble

carpenter who fell in love with Helwise, daughter of Sir Ferdinand Pennington. The infuriated father bribed Tom, the court jester, to do away with him, which he did, cutting off the man's head to prove his mission accomplished.

King Henry VIII—Windsor, Berkshire

The ghost of Henry VIII is one of the more pathetic spectres of Windsor, seen, but more usually heard, walking in the cloisters of the Deanery. After a hunting accident, Henry was left with an injured leg which never properly healed and caused him a great deal of pain towards the end of his days. Gout and his excess weight aggravated his injury, so that he dragged his ulcerated leg and often groaned as he walked, in much the same way as his ghost is heard groaning and limping in the cloisters.

Lulu von Herkomer—Bushey, Hertfordshire

Lulu von Herkomer, wife of Baron von Herkomer, is reputed to haunt Bushey Film Studios, where their country mansion once stood. It was pulled down to make way for the pioneer film venture, though Lulu's ghost was already in residence when the wreckers moved in. She stood her ground—in a spectral sense—and, soon after the first picture was begun, 'a luminous blue lady' stalked across the unlit set, frightening two young starlets and scaring a producer out of his wits.

Vincent Herman—Brooklands, Weybridge, Surrey

Though positive identity is difficult, this is believed to be another of the ghosts from the early days of motor-sport—Vincent Herman, crushed as his car overturned in September 1907, the year the Brooklands circuit was opened. His clothing is little more than a dark blur, his goggles partly conceal his face, a close-fitting, flying-style helmet hides much of his head, yet some are convinced that the first man to die on the old track haunts what was once the famous Railway Straight.

Herne The Hunter—Windsor Great Park, Berkshire

'A tall, dark figure of hideous physiognomy and strange attire helmed with a huge pair of antlers . . .' is how historical novelist Harrison Ainsworth described Herne. His ghost is said to be one of the most elusive and persistent in all England, having haunted Windsor Forest since Henry VIII found him guilty of poaching Royal deer, which caused Herne to hang himself from an oak tree in Home Park. Early accounts of the haunting suggest a more formidable figure that caused cattle to fall dead and trees to wither. There is some confusion about the date of Herne's existence, since there was also a forest warden named Herne who served Richard II.

Tom Hewson—Harpham, Humberside

There are conflicting stories as to how a drummer boy, Tom Hewson, came to drown in the overgrown well which he haunts behind the church at Harpham. Was he pushed by Squire St Quintin (whose family owned Harpham from the fourteenth to the nineteenth centuries), or did he accidentally fall while watching the soldiers at archery practice? Whichever way it happened young Tom's mother, a local witch, decreed her son's ghost would forever drum the Squire's descendants to their graves, beating a long roll on his drum before the death of any of the St Quintin family.

Reverend Samson Hieron—White Horse, Chilham, Kent

In the seventeenth century this pub was the vicarage neighbouring St Mary's Church, of which the Reverend Hieron was the incumbent. Although Vicar Hieron was sacked for his non-conformist preachings, he was a good man and, when he died in 1677, he was buried in the churchyard next door. All the same, the benign old reverend gentleman's ghost—grey-haired, black-gowned and gaitered—remains in residence to this day and is often still seen warming himself in front of the massive inglenook fire, though his old home is now one of the most picturesque of Kent's 'old worlde' inns.

Edward Higgins—Royal George Hotel, Knutsford, Cheshire

This clever, even courteous, highwayman went to the gallows on 7 November 1767, leaving a wife and five children and a full confession of his crimes, which included murder. He also left a ghost which haunts the Royal George, the place in which he made some of his richest pickings among Georgian society, by whom he was accepted—unrecognised by day—as a gentleman.

Another haunting at the Royal George is a phantom coach, with ghostly coachmen, complete with the noise of iron-rimmed wheels on the cobbles and the sounding of the post horn.

Abbess St Hilda—Whitby, North Yorkshire

The Saxon Abbess, Hilda, established her abbey at Whitby in AD 657. It survived 200 years until sacked by the Danes. The ruins she is reputed to haunt are of the Benedictine monastery built by the Normans on the same site. Her ghost, wrapped in a shroud, has been seen in one of the highest windows of the ruins, viewed from the west end of Whitby Churchyard, looking north.

Whitby also has a ghost of a murdered simpleton called Goosey, a name he earned after accepting, and winning, a wager to eat a whole goose at one sitting.

Sir Rowland Hill—Kidderminster Telephone Exchange, Worcestershire

The father of the Post Office, Sir Rowland Hill, was a Worcestershire boy, so it's not surprising there are reports that his ghost has been seen—and heard—in Kidderminster, the town of his birth. Night operators at the Kidderminster Telephone Exchange believe they are being haunted by the shadowy figure of Sir Rowland, who introduced sweeping post office reforms in eighteenth-century Britain, as well as successfully launching the penny postal system.

Squire Hilliard—Brixham, Devon

This sixteenth-century squire, who lived at The Black Horse, in Higher Brixham, remonstrated with his son when the boy announced his plans to marry a local country lass. Ambitious for his son, he put pressure on the girl and her family to ensure she married somebody else, and it was no small shock for the boy when, by accident, he saw his girl leaving the church after her hastily arranged wedding. Insane with rage he hanged himself from the nearest tree, using his horse's reins as a noose.

The tragedy has left its ghosts: a remorseful squire seeking his son to ask forgiveness and the clatter of horses hooves as young Hilliard's phantom horse returns home riderless.

Anne Hinchfield—Montpelier Road, Ealing, London

A picture published in Andrew Green's book *Our Haunted Kingdom* (Wolfe) suggests that the ghost of twelve-year-old Anne Hinchfield haunted 16 Montpelier Road, Ealing W5 before the depressing old house was demolished. Mr Green's own photograph of the deserted house, taken in 1944, shows what could be the ghostly image of a girl in the top left-hand window of the building, from the top of which Anne jumped to her death in 1887.

Lady Elizabeth Hoby—Bisham Abbey, Buckinghamshire

Lady Hoby, confidant of Queen Elizabeth I, was a scholarly woman who had no patience with stupidity. She was twice married, had six children and lived to be eighty-one. She haunts her old home of Bisham Abbey in several ways—with shuffling footsteps, sobbing hysterically, or, more often than not, she is seen walking (or gliding) with a basin floating before her in which she continually washes her hands. Legend says she is washing off the blood of her son, William, who was slow and untidy in his studies, and whom she thrashed so severely that he died.

Tom Hoggett—Great North Road, North Yorkshire

Hoggett, the highwayman, has a pool named after him, close to the A1. It's the place at which he tried to escape his captors, but, in the pitch darkness of a stormy, moonless night, he fell into the pond and drowned. The ghostly highwayman seen patrolling the Great North Road, between Boroughbridge and Scotch Corner, is the shade of Tom Hoggett, a fast moving figure in an ankle-length coat with a cape and a bull's-eye lantern.

Earl of Holland—New Inn, St Neots, Huntingdonshire

Lord Holland was one of those executed after the second phase of the Civil War ended in defeat for the Royalists. Before he was removed to the Tower, he, and a number of officers who served under him, was held prisoner at the New Inn, which is where the Earl's ghost walks, 'a tall, slender figure with an aloof appearance and dressed in an ankle-length cloak'.

Ada Holmes—The Crowtree, Sunderland, Tyne and Wear

Mrs Ada Holmes was licensee of the tiny Crowtree Inn in Sunderland's town centre for more than thirty years. She died aged eighty-six and was given a funeral at the nearby parish church which would have done justice to a judge. That was in 1965, since when the ghost of the frail old landlady, grey-haired, bespectacled and wearing her favourite multicoloured dress, with a shawl or cardigan round her shoulders, has been back many times, usually in the evening, after closing time.

Queen Catherine (Howard)—Hampton Court Palace, Middlesex

This grand-daughter of the 2nd Duke of Norfolk was Queen of England at twenty-one, having secretly married Henry VIII in 1540, to become his fifth wife. At the time she was already betrothed to Thomas Culpepper, a relationship she foolishly tried to continue after marrying the King. She died for her indiscretions on Tower Green on 13 February 1542. While under arrest at Hampton Court, Queen Catherine made a bold attempt to save herself, breaking free of her guards and running along the corridor leading to the chapel where Henry VIII was at prayers.

There she beat on the door, hopeful of pleading for mercy. But the guards dragged her away, screaming, while Henry continued praying. It is here, in what is now officially called the Haunted Gallery, that the distraught ghost of the young Queen has been witnessed re-enacting that last desperate bid for her husband's forgiveness.

Lady Mary Howard—Okehampton Castle, Devon

This lady is much maligned by a remarkable seventeenth-century legend in which she is described as 'the wicked Lady Howard' who murdered three husbands and two children. For her crimes, she was 'doomed to a fearful penance', part of which was to drive nightly over the moor in a coach made of the bones of her dead husbands. A deputy keeper at Okehampton Castle has seen her ghost, but not in the bony coach. The historical facts show her to be a kindly and respectable woman, far from evil, four times married, with two daughters. On the other hand, her father, Sir John Fitz of Fitzford, Tavistock, was a dissolute man, guilty of two murders, but without a ghost.

Dr Michael Hudson—Woodcroft Manor, Huntingdonshire

This chaplain to Charles I, and leader of the Royalists in the vicinity of Woodcroft Manor, would not surrender when besieged there by Roundheads in 1648. One by one his courageous little band was slaughtered, leaving only the doctor facing six enemy pikemen. Ignoring his cry for mercy they forced him over the battlements and hacked off his hands as he clung for his life. He was hauled from the moat and butchered. Against a background of clashing swords and pikes, his voice is still heard shouting 'Mercy' and 'Quarter'.

William Hunter—The Swan, Brentwood, Essex

William Hunter was only nineteen when he was burned for his Protestant beliefs on the morning of 25 March 1555. He was one of at least 300 heretics condemned to die during the five years of Mary Tudor's reign. William spent his last night at The Swan, during which he had a dream about his execution, all of which happened in more or less the way he foresaw it. His ghost has been known to make nightly visits to The Swan where he had his premonitory dream. Furthermore, plates with religious inscriptions will not stay for long on the walls. Similarly, furniture is mysteriously moved and lights switched on.

Lady Ursula Hynde—Madingley Hall, Cambridgeshire

Lady Ursula was wife of Sir John Hynde who built Madingley Hall, a Tudor house among trees on the outskirts of Cambridge. Her son, Francis, continued the building after his father's death, adding, among other things, a hammer-beam roof removed from the church of St Etheureda at Histon. Such violation was too much for the old lady; her unhappy ghost walks Madingley and its grounds, wringing her hands in sorrow at her son's sacrilegious behaviour. A war-time soldier saw her walk across the courtyard, while an *au pair* girl saw her, in 1951, in her turret bedroom.

I

Brother Ignatius—Elm, Cambridgeshire

Brother Ignatius belonged to a monastic order in the Fen country more than 750 years ago. It was his responsibility to keep watch and warn the community of impending floods, by tolling a bell. He once failed to do so and the waters swept across the low lands and engulfed the village of Elm, drowning a number of the brothers. Ignatius, the bell-ringer, has not rested since, tolling a phantom bell whenever there is a death in the village.

Prince Imperial of France—The Angel, Guildford

The Prince Imperial stayed at The Angel in 1876, sleeping in a double room on the first floor overlooking Guildford's cobbled high street. It is Room 1, now named after him. The ghost that has been seen there, visible in the 7ft high mirror of the large wardrobe, is thought to be his, in army uniform of the late nineteenth century. The figure was of a middle-aged man, with dark hair, a gaucho-moustache and a very compelling expression in the eyes. It remained 'reflected' in the mirror for half-an-hour when seen in 1970, long enough for the witness to do a sketch on a red paper napkin, the only thing available.

Elizabeth Ingilby—Ripley Castle, Harrogate, North Yorkshire

Elizabeth Ingilby, who became the Nun of Ghent, haunts Ripley, home of the Ingilbys for more than 600 years. Her portrait hangs at the top of the main staircase, while her ghostly figure flits along the castle corridors, rousing sleeping guests with a rap on the door, but pausing only if the occupant calls to her to come in.

Sir Henry Irving—Bradford, West Yorkshire

His real name was John Henry Brodribb, son of a Somerset tradesman, who, without doubt, became the brightest star in the theatrical world of Victorian England. His ghost is believed to walk the boards of the Theatre Royal, Bradford, where, after a performance of *Becket*, he collapsed and died on 13 October 1905.

Mary Isaac—The Horns, Crucifix Lane, London SE1

This is the ghost of a little girl, an eight–ten-year-old who once lived at The Horns, probably in Victorian times. She is heard crying and calling desperately for her mother, who, seemingly, died and left the child an orphan. Mary died also, but could not find her mother, so returned to The Horns in spirit form to look for her. Canon Pearce-Higgins of the Church Fellowship for Psychical Study was asked to free the pub of this ghost, which he did, working with the well known medium, Mr Donald Page. Furthermore, they discovered The Horns has another ghost, that of an old lady who haunts in an upstairs room.

Rabbi Isaacs—Norwich, Norfolk

The spirit of Rabbi Isaacs is said to linger in the Tudor house in the centre of Norwich known as 'Old Jewry', a name suggestive of the fact that a synagogue once stood on the site. It was part of the Jewish quarter destroyed by fire late in the thirteenth century. Legend has it that the Rabbi, for some obscure reason, murdered his wife, buried her body in the crypt of the synagogue and then fired the building. Excavation in the 1880s revealed burnt earth and the bones of a long-dead woman.

Queen Isabella—Castle Rising, Norfolk

Known in history as the 'She-wolf of France', this ambitious wife of Edward II, mistress of Roger Mortimer, is said to haunt the ruins of Castle Rising, as well as the darkest depths of Nottingham Castle. She was depressed and often violent while in confinement in Norfolk, after the execution of Mortimer. At times, her ghost is seen clambering on the grass-covered mounds, walking on top of the crumbling walls, moreover, it is heard shouting and laughing like a maniac. She was buried in the churchyard at Greyfriars, London, with the heart of her murdered husband on her bosom. Seemingly conscience-stricken, her ghost walks in the ruined churchyard, which is also the haunt of another husband-killer, Lady Alice Hungerford, beautiful second wife of Sir Edward, whom she poisoned in 1523.

'Mrs It'—Yattendon, Berkshire

Exorcism has put an end, at least for the present, to the haunting by 'Mrs It' at this old Berkshire rectory. The wife of the rector living there at the end of World War II described her as grey-black, 'like smoke and of the same consistency'. She wore a bonnet, a shawl over a dress of watered silk, and carried a basket. She was always in a hurry. The whole family encountered her in various parts of house and garden and because they felt she was such a charming old lady called her 'Mrs It' as a courtesy. Family research suggests she was the unmarried sister of the Reverend Puller, a rector there in the 1720s.

J

Peg-leg Jack—Chatham, Kent

This is the name given to the ghost of a wooden-legged sailor of Nelson's navy, seen stumping along with his peg-leg towards Room 34 of Cumberland Block, the oldest part of Chatham Naval Barracks. It is thought to be the ghost of a sentry who was killed by escaping French prisoners during the Napoleonic Wars. They beat him to death as he was going to wake his relief, who was late for duty. The sighting is officially on record in the duty officer's log book. The entry reads: 'Ghost reported seen during middle watch'.

Spring-heel Jack—Barnes Common, London

He could leap over houses, take walls and fences in his giant stride. He was even impervious to bullets fired by army riflemen. For the best part of a hundred years, he terrorised town and country, making a first horrific appearance near Barnes Common early last century. 'He could leap 30 feet at a bound', reported *The Morning Post* 'and was clearly no ordinary mortal, if indeed he were of this world at all . . . he was a bogey, the terror of whom kept women indoors after dark.' He was last seen in 1904, leaping along William Henry Street, Everton, and never apprehended.

Captain Jacques—Royal Anchor Hotel, Liphook, Hampshire

Captain Jacques was a Frenchman who deserted the sea to become a highwayman on the old Portsmouth Road. He had some of his lushest pickings on the ten curvaceous miles between Petersfield and the Royal Anchor at Liphook, where he was eventually cornered by the excisemen and shot down trying to escape. Room 6 was the scene of his dramatic end and has been the place where his ghost is seen stepping through a concealed door at the side of the big fireplace, the same door he was frantically trying to open when the excisemen caught up with him.

James, Duke of Monmouth—Sedgemoor, Somerset

Monmouth was beheaded on 15 July 1685, nine days after losing the last battle fought on English soil—the disaster of Sedgemoor. Perhaps had the Duke not ridden off into the foggy dawn of 6 July, his army of Somerset peasants would have fought on even more stoutly. As it was, their gallant stand cost them more than a thousand dead, according to Macauley's history, though a manuscript in Weston Zoyland church says but 300 died fighting. Whatever the slaughter, Sedgemoor left an army of ghosts, and among them a phantom Cavalier horseman, thought by many to be the rebel Duke himself.

Lady Jane—Hope, Clwyd, North Wales

'Young and Beautiful' is how the legend-makers describe this ghost, said to haunt Plas Teg, a seventeenth-century house near Hope. It is the phantom Lady Jane, loved by two men from neighbouring Welsh families, both of whom so desperately wanted to marry her that they fought a duel to settle the issue. Not being a fairy story things didn't work out for Jane the way she had hoped; the man she really loved was killed, causing her to commit suicide by leaping into the well. In trying to rescue her, the victor of the fight fell in also and was drowned.

William Jarman—Little Gaddesden, Hertfordshire

Jarman, a church warden, lived during the eighteenth century in the Elizabethan Manor House at Little Gaddesden. He hanged himself there after being rejected by the heiress of Ashbridge, a neighbouring estate, once the home of the earls of Bridgewater. Since his suicide, Jarman's ghost has been seen near the village duck pond, which, before development, was just across the green, opposite the manor gate. There are some who say he drowned himself in the pond, after waiting in vain for his would-be sweetheart.

Mary Jay—Widecombe, Devon

Near the High Tor Inn, north of Widecombe-in-the-Moor is Mary Jay's grave, the burial place of an eighteenth-century orphan from the workhouse, who hanged herself when she found she was pregnant by her farmhand lover. A phantom figure, without feet or legs, has been seen stooping at the graveside, but a dark blanket over head and shoulders prevents positive identity. Flowers are frequently to be found on the grave, although it is not certain who puts them there.

Old Jeffrey—Epworth Rectory, Lincolnshire

Old Jeffrey, more accurately described as a poltergeist, began to haunt the Wesley family at Epworth, in 1716. John Wesley, later to become leader and founder of the Methodist movement, was thirteen at the time of the disturbances, which were loud knocks and deep groans, as well as heavy footsteps going up and down stairs and people being forcibly pushed by unseen hands. Most of the Wesley's nineteen children were adolescent while Old Jeffrey was active and Hetty, one of the daughters saw 'something like a man' in a loose nightshirt, on the stairs. Only the dog showed any fear of this ghost, which was assumed to be a former occupant, known as 'Old Jeffrey' who had died in the rectory.

Judge Jeffreys—1st Baron of Wem—Chard, Somerset

George Jeffreys left his bloody mark on south-west England with a vengeance. He made those who supported Monmouth pay dearly with slavery, transportation, flogging, or execution. As though loath to leave the scene of some of his most bestial punishments, the seventeenth-century Lord High Chancellor still haunts many of the places at which he conducted his Bloody Assizes. There is an upper room of Choughs Hotel, Chard, in which he slept and which his ghost is said to frequent. In Taunton, too, there is a haunted bedroom at The Castle, again a room once used by the Hanging Judge. Until recently, the ruined Norman castle at Lydford, on the edge of Dartmoor, was the gloomy place his phantom haunted most frequently. In the last decade, the Great House at Lyme Regis has been having repeated visits from the spectral judge, wearing his robes, wig and black cap.

Jimmy—Camfield Place, Hatfield, Hertfordshire

Jimmy is the ghost of a cocker spaniel, once the pet of the younger son of Barbara Cartland, the romantic novelist. In 1955, the dog had to be put down and, soon afterwards, curious things began to happen, particularly at their other dogs' feeding time. While they ate, they seemed to eye something that was not there, occasionally barking or growling at it. Then Jimmy's ghost began to materialise and was seen about the house by both Miss Cartland and her maid. Once, when Miss Cartland tried to edge Jimmy out of the way with her foot, the dog just vanished.

Sir Strange Jocelyn—Hyde Hall, Sawbridgeworth, Hertfordshire

Sir Strange, non-conformist owner of Hyde Hall, had some unorthodox views about religion which got him into lively arguments. The suggestion that caused him the biggest conflict was that he should be buried, when the time came, in the parish churchyard, with his favourite horse. He was turned down and, eventually, he and his mount were buried in the grounds of Hyde Hall in the same grave. From time to time, Sir Strange's spectre rides on his phantom favourite along the drive leading to his old home which is now a girls' school.

John the Jibber—Marsden Grotto, near Sunderland, Tyne and Wear

John the Jibber was a smuggler, one of the Marsden gang using the Grotto to land cargoes of contraband shipped into Marsden Bay. His agonising end came after betraying the gang to the coastguards. Had it not been for Peter Allan, a hermit who lived in the grotto with his wife and eight children, every one of the gang might have been taken red-handed. As it was, Allan, sensing treachery, fired his pistol as a warning to the smugglers' lugger, lying off shore. For informing, John the Jibber paid with his life. He was left to starve, trussed up in a barrel hoisted to the cavern roof. His piteous death-groans have echoed through the grotto for more than a century.

Dean Jones—Blenheim Palace, Oxfordshire

Dean Jones, the 1st Duke of Marlborough's chaplain, has the double distinction of being the ghost of Blenheim Palace *and* of haunting the room—small and simple by Blenheim standards—where Sir Winston Churchill was born. The Dean is reputed to have haunted what was originally his bedroom, vainly searching, it appears, for a book he lent to the first Duchess. Because of his clerical garb, he was described as the 'black ghost'. It seems Sir Winston's premature birth in that room, in 1874, has, in some way, helped to exorcise the phantom Dean, because, since the palace was re-opened to the public, there have been no disturbances.

Harry Jones—Malmesbury, Wiltshire

Harry Jones was, for forty years, landlord of The Kings Arms and once Mayor of Malmesbury. Everybody knew him by his Edwardian mode of dress which never changed with the times; he always sported a brightly coloured waistcoat under a long, loose fitting coat, turned-up trousers and a tall, straight-brimmed hat. Since his death, in 1920, his ghost has remained at the pub that had been his since 1880. Beer taps have been turned off and lights switched on by unseen hands, thought to be Harry's, and ghostly heavy breathing is heard in the bedroom where he died.

Brother Joseph—Little Hempston, Devon

This ghost, of a hunch-backed monk of French origin from the old abbey at Buckfast, haunts The Pig and Whistle Inn at Little Hempston, thought once to have been a roadside lodging place for brethren and pilgrims journeying to the Abbey from the coast. Brother Joseph's life-time interest in the place was a local woman, whom he met there almost daily, covering the six miles from

Buckfast on horseback. If disturbed in his lovemaking, he would make a quick exit via a tunnel which led to an adjoining chapel.

K

Herbert Kay—Forest Gate, London

Herbert Kay, a fifty-two-year-old dentist, who died when a wartime landmine exploded outside the Princess Alice in London's East End, is thought to be the ghost which caused havoc at the pub in 1975. He was seen to walk through walls, bang doors, shake beds, drink beer and flood the pub by turning on the beer taps. Those who saw him before he was finally exorcised described him as 6ft tall and 'well built'.

Emily Kaye—Pevensey, Sussex

Poor Emily Kaye—she was chopped up and burned by her lover in a bungalow, once the officers' house of the coastguard at Pevensey Bay. That was in 1924, since when, her ghost, a tall figure in a long white gown, has been seen on The Crumbles, a stretch of marshy foreshore near Langley Point.

Bishop Thomas Ken—Longleat, Wiltshire

It is said Bishop Ken of Bath and Wells went to Longleat for dinner, and stayed as a religious refugee for twenty years. In fact he stayed a great deal longer, since his ghost still haunts the Bishop Ken Library, where he remained as a guest of his great friend the first Viscount Weymouth, who sympathised with the Bishop's refusal to swear allegiance to William III, even though he had been chaplain to the Princess of Orange. He is supposed to revisit the library named after him, particularly on 15 March, his birthday.

Captain William Kidd RN—Wapping, London

For killing a seaman on his own ship, Captain Kidd died at Execution Dock, Wapping, in 1707, hanged and left for three high tides to wash over his body. At the time of his trial, many believed the charge against him was trumped-up, that he was in fact being sentenced for his acts of piracy in the Indian Ocean. Either way, his ghost was reported soon after his death near Execution Dock, a shadowy figure which partly emerged from the river and moved upstream before submerging again. More recently there have been accounts of it appearing at Wapping Old Stairs.

Ned King—Hurst Green, near Blackburn, Lancashire

Ned King was a ruggedly handsome man in his twenties who cut a dashing figure in white-ruffled shirt, gold-trimmed scarlet coat, white breeches and knee-high black boots, the working clothes for an eighteenth-century highwayman. His last shoot-out with the troopers was in the hayloft behind the Punch Bowl at Hurst Green. Eventually taken away in chains, King was later gibbetted beside Gallows Lane, a short walk from his favourite hide-out. It would be disloyal if King's ghost was to haunt anywhere but there, though he is described as 'a bad-tempered ghost causing much disturbance when things don't go his way', so much so that in 1942 a priest from nearby Stonyhurst College performed a partially successful exorcism.

L

Bishop Lacy—Chudleigh, Devon

Edmund Lacy, fourteenth-century Bishop of Exeter, seems to have left behind a ghost which haunts the inn which bears his name at Chudleigh. There is certainly a cowled figure, seen in what was once the bishop's summer residence, the oldest building in Chudleigh, being the only place to survive a devastating fire which swept the village in 1807.

Marie Lairre—Borley, Essex

During the half century that Borley Rectory in Essex has been in and out of the newspapers as 'the most haunted place in Britain', spectral activity there has included a coach and horses, the spirits of two allegedly murdered people, a phantom cat, footsteps, ringing bells, voices and, above all, a nun. Although scores of psychic investigators have flocked there and numerous seances have been held on the site of the cold, gloomy Victorian house, which, in February 1939, was gutted by fire, the who or what of Borley remain unanswered. Without doubt, the most repetitive manifestation and the most substantial is the nun, seen as far back as 1885. It is suggested that she may be Marie Lairre, a young French nun murdered by drowning at Borley in 1667.

Percy Lambert—Brooklands, Weybridge, Surrey

Lambert was a hero of Brooklands motor-racing track in the days before World War I. Motoring was still in its infancy when he became the first man to cover over 100 miles in 60 minutes. Eight months later, in October 1913, he was killed doing the, then, shattering speed of 114·23 mph. Brooklands is now a ghost track, the steep concrete banking broken, overgrown, and little Percy is one of its ghosts, a helmeted, goggled figure at the wheel of an ancient Talbot. The shape is vague, though the engine sound is unmistakable, travelling about 40 yards along the old track before fading away.

Ann Lamplugh—Irton Hall, Cumbria

The lady in black who walks one of the rooms at Irton is thought to be Ann Lamplugh, remorseful wife of John Irton, who refused sanctuary to the fugitive King Henry VI, fleeing from the Yorkist army after his defeat at Tewkesbury. The battle-weary Henry spent a painful night hiding from his pursuers in a great oak tree, after he had been turned away from the hall, an inhospitable act which seems still to trouble the conscience of Mistress Irton.

Sir William Langhorne—Charlton House, London

Sir William made his fortune trading with the East, earned himself a knighthood and the Governorship of Madras. With part of his wealth he bought Charlton House as 'an asylum for his old age', as well as for the fine view across Blackheath. Optimistically, he married twice, but died, aged eighty-five, without an heir. However, he did leave a ghost, which haunts most actively in the corridors of the old home (now a community centre), lurking on the stairs, turning bedroom door knobs and looking in presumably still hoping to find the right woman.

Archbishop Laud—St John's, Oxford

William Laud, son of a Reading clothier, became Archbishop of Canterbury and ended his days in the Tower of London, accused of treason. He was eventually beheaded in 1645, since when his ghost has been reported rolling his head on the floor of St John's College, Oxford, where he was educated, and where, some years later, became chancellor of the university. The Archbishop's ghost has been reported at Hampton Court, as well as Oxford.

T. E. Lawrence—Cloud's Hill, Dorset

The unmistakable sound of a Brough Superior motor-bike being kick-started in the quietness before dawn, is said to be part of the phenomena of Cloud's Hill. This is where the spectre of Lawrence of Arabia has been seen in Arab dress, outside the neat, white-painted cottage that was his.

Lizzie Lawton—The Angel Inn, Lyme Regis, Dorset

Old Mrs Lawton is a very jealous ghost. She loved her pub, The Angel at Lyme Regis, and can't stand anyone else running the place, especially women. Since she died, this little old lady, dressed like Queen Victoria, with her hair in a bun and always wearing a white apron, has been back several times to have a look at the various landlords who have succeeded her. Says a near neighbour who knew her in the flesh: 'She was a lovely woman. Very kind and very old fashioned ... She never wanted to leave the pub.'

Widow Leaky—Minehead, Somerset

The ghost of Widow Leaky was famous in Somerset in the seventeenth century. She was known as 'the Whistling Spectre', since she appeared in the street whistling in a spine-prickling way. Her son was a Minehead shipowner and she even haunted his ships when at sea, standing before the mast, whistling. Her hauntings were, in the beginning, mischievous, but later malicious, all aimed at drawing attention to a terrible wrong to which she was a party during her lifetime, namely the undisclosed murder by a brother-in-law of his illegitimate child.

David Leany—Glad-Wish Wood, Sussex

Nineteen-years-old David Leany was a farmhand hanged in 1825 for a murder that didn't happen. He was a lodger at the Burwash cottage of Benjamin Russell, the man he was accused of killing. While both men were poaching in Glad-Wish Wood, Russell died of a heart attack, but, within twenty-four hours, village gossips put the rope round Leany's neck by hinting at an affair with Russell's wife. As he was about to hang, Leany shouted: 'I shall return to haunt these people who have hounded me to my death'. And return to Glad-Wish Wood he has, a ragged thing that plucks at its throat as it blunders through the undergrowth.

Jane Leeson—Abthorpe, Northamphire

Jane Leeson is well remembered in the village of Abthorpe and not only because she left money for the church, and money with which to build a free school. She left a ghost too, which haunts the derelict manor house where she lived in the seventeenth century. Her perambulations cause the doors to creak, and, on still, quiet nights one can hear her silk gown rustling as she walks.

Another ghost seen in the vicinity is that of a monk in grey Franciscan habit, lending support to the suggestion that there was once a monastic cell hereabouts.

Sir Piers Legh—Lyme Park, Cheshire

Sir Piers died of his wounds after the battle of Agincourt, in 1422. As was his wish, the body was brought back to Lyme Park, the ancestral home, for burial. Yet, long after its interment on Knight's Low, a ghostly funeral procession was often seen moving slowly along the drive beside the lake. Over the years that haunting has faded, until today the apparition is not of the cortege bearing Sir Piers, but of a lone woman mourner walking with bowed head. This sorrowing all-white figure, known locally as Blanche, is not his wife but the knight's secret mistress. She died of grief when news of his death reached her.

Dan Leno—Theatre Royal, London

Dan Leno, Victorian comedian and champion clog dancer, was vouched for by another famous comedian, Stanley Lupino, as an active phantom of the Theatre Royal, Drury Lane. Stanley Lupino, spending the night in what had been Dan Leno's favourite dressing room, saw the deathly white, but unmistakable, features of Leno in the make-up mirror. Lupino rushed from the theatre and spent the rest of the night at the Globe Theatre down the street.

Charles John Kean, actor-manager, and son of the great Edmund Kean, has also put in a ghostly appearance at Drury Lane.

Armine L'Estrange—Hunstanton, Norfolk

As Armine L'Estrange lay on her death bed in 1766, she made a last request, that her Persian carpet, presented by the Shah, should always remain in the family. Faithfully, her servants packed it up into a wooden chest, which was manhandled into the attic and forgotten. Rediscovered long years later, by somebody who had never heard of Armine's dying wish, the carpet was cut up and distributed among the villagers. That caused the angry ghost of Armine to create so much terror, that the pieces of carpet were hastily collected up and stitched together again, to placate her.

Ladies of Levens—Kendal, Cumbria

The Bagot family live with three ghosts and 800 years of history behind the walls of Levens Hall. 'The ghosts are to amuse, alarm or entertain', says the guidebook, depending on a visitors' nerves or imagination. For the Pink Lady, strong nerves are not necessary. Only her clothes, her mob cap and pink skirt looped up at the waist, hint that she may be a lady's maid left over from the eighteenth century. The Grey Lady is more chilling, the gypsy of the 'Curse of Levens', with lank hair and naked feet and an unnerving habit of walking in front of cars. The other ghost? That is a small black dog, with bright eyes and a woolly coat so life-like that it gets chased for real by the other dogs of Levens.

Field Marshal Lord Ligonier—Cobham, Surrey

Jean Louis Ligonier was a tall, well built French Huguenot who came to England in the mid-eighteenth century to escape religious persecution. He lived at Cobham Place, became Commander in Chief of the British forces, and survived the battle of Malplaquet, despite twenty-two bullet holes in his clothes. Although he was buried locally when he died in 1770, it is said his ghost is still active on the Portsmouth Road at Pines Hill, Cobham. The figure is described as tall and luminous in an army field-coat, staring vacantly ahead from empty eye sockets.

Lady Lisgar—Husbands Bosworth, Leicestershire

Lady Lisgar, a Protestant widow who, in 1881, married Sir Francis Fortescue-Turvile, the head of the Catholic family who, for centuries, have lived at Husbands Bosworth, is the ghost at Bosworth Hall. She refused to permit a priest to give the last rites to a dying maidservant, and is damned to haunt forever.

Dame Alice Lisle—The Eclipse Inn, Winchester, Hampshire

On 2 September 1685, Dame Alice was beheaded in The Square at

Winchester for unwittingly hiding three men on the run after the battle of Sedgemoor. This old lady was tried as a traitor by Judge Jefferies and sentenced to be burned at the stake, a terrible end which she escaped due to the intervention of the Bishop of Winchester. After the axe had fallen, hundreds of ordinary Hampshire men and women escorted the body to Ellingham, where it was laid to rest. But her ghost has not rested. To this day it haunts The Eclipse, which stands at the corner of The Square, and was the building in which she spent her last night.

Catherine Tylney Long—Wanstead Park, London

This sweet young thing shares her Wanstead Park haunt with a Royal ghost—the illustrious Elizabeth Tudor. In the 1820s, she was considered one of the richest heiresses in all England, until she lost everything to an unscrupulous admirer. The shock of being suddenly deprived of her home and inheritance so unbalanced her mind that she killed herself, leaving a remorseful ghost as a warning to others not to heed glib-tongued adventurers.

Major Ralph Longworth—St Michael's on Wyre, Lancashire

This old soldier could never rest peacefully in his grave after a life of warring with the Royalist armies, first at Preston, then at Wigan Lane, and, finally, as a silver-haired major in Colonel Kirkby's militia. Old St Michael's Hall, where he lived, was constantly haunted by this veteran, until demolished in the 1860s. Apart from moving the furniture, banging doors and clattering pots and pans, he was seen parading in the lane outside the hall, but there have been no reports of the ghostly major since the vicar and parish priest performed a combined exorcism.

Lord Lovell—Minster Lovell, Oxford

This fifteenth-century member of the Lovell family, the 9th Baron, gave his support to the 1487 rebellion, led by John de la Pole, Earl of Lincoln, against Henry VII. After the King's victory at the battle of Stoke, his lordship went into hiding. He locked himself in a concealed room at Minster Lovell Hall, and was attended by only one loyal retainer. When that servant died, Lord Lovell died too, slowly and painfully—of starvation. The hall is now a ruin, haunted by the ghost of his lordship, whose skeleton (so it is presumed) was discovered in 1718, sitting at a table, with a skeleton hound at its feet.

Sir James Lowther—Lowther Castle, Cumbria

Sir James, the first Lord Lonsdale, was as much an eccentric as a ghost as he was during his lifetime. He didn't wait for his funeral to end before starting his supernatural activities, which took the form of a violent, unseen force knocking the praying clergyman off his knees and causing the pall bearers to stagger like drunken men as they carried the swaying coffin. Shortly afterwards, the peace of Lowther Castle was disrupted by loud bangings, slamming doors and running footsteps. Local inhabitants reported seeing his spectral lordship sitting on the box of a coach and six, rampaging around the countryside.

Lucette—Clayton le Moors, Lancashire

Lucette was a young French governess employed by the Petre family at their Dunkenhalgh Park home in the eighteenth century. She was loved by the children and the family, until her blatant affair with a dashing redcoat officer she met at a family Christmas party. By the following mid-summer, it was obvious she was pregnant and, despairing of her soldier-lover returning to marry her as promised, she drowned herself in the river Hyndburn, which flows through the park. Her lifeless body was found under the old stone bridge, now called Boggart Bridge because it is there that Lucette's ghost is seen walking by the river under the trees, disappearing on reaching the water's edge.

Lady Luvibund—Goodwin Sands, off Deal, Kent

The *Lady Luvibund*, a schooner, was deliberately grounded on the Goodwin Sands by a jealous first mate. For Captain Simon Reid it was a honeymoon trip. He and his bride were celebrating in the skipper's cabin when the mate, secretly in love with the young wife, swung the wheel and sent the ship crunching onto the quicksands. By first light on 14 February 1748, she had been sucked down with all hands, below the Goodwins, gone forever. But not quite forever. A ghost ship identical to the *Lady Luvibund* has been seen four times since—at fifty-year intervals, each time on 13 February, the night of the disaster.

M

Charles Macklin—Theatre Royal, London

Macklin (or McLaughlin to give him his real name) is thought to be another of the Drury Lane ghosts. A tall, lean hatchet-faced wraith, reported from time to time crossing in front of what used to be the pit, could be the quarrelsome Irish actor, who, in 1735, killed Thomas Hallam, a fellow actor. Hallam, who died as the result of Macklin jabbing a stick into his eyeball during an argument, has never been seen to haunt, whereas Macklin's ghost is seen in the early evening, at about the time the quarrel is believed to have happened.

The Mad Monk—Little Haldon, Devon

A ghost with fourteenth-century origins haunts the ruined chapel at the roadside, opposite Little Haldon golf course. It is known locally as the Mad Monk, who persuaded travellers to enter his cell to give them absolution, then murdered and robbed them, before throwing the bodies into the nearby holy well of Our Lady.

Baldwin Malet—Poyntington, Dorset

In the little church at Poyntington, on the Somerset-Dorset border, are the arms of the Malet family and below them these words: 'Baldwin Malet, second sonne of Sir Thomas Malet dyed in the King's service the third of June, AD 1646, in the twentieth yeare of his age'. With a sparsely armed band of rustics, he tried to halt a Roundhead force marching on Wincanton. In less than an hour Malet and his simple followers were bloody corpses in a water meadow. For fear of plague, their bodies were hastily covered with earth, and the grass-covered mounds—and a ghostly band of headless peasants—can still be seen today.

Sir Geoffrey de Mandeville—East Barnet, Hertfordshire

Sir Geoffrey, rebel Earl of Essex, died fighting in Suffolk, was buried in London, and haunts an East Barnet recreation ground. Every sixth Christmas Eve, at an hour before midnight, he is reputed to walk on Oak Hill 'clad in armour, a red cloak and spurs'. Reasons why his ghost treads this northern outpost of suburban London have faded down the centuries since 1141, when the over-generous King Stephen approved of Sir Geoffrey as Sheriff and Justice of not only London, but of Middlesex, Essex and Hertfordshire.

Lord Marney—Tiptree, Essex

The first Lord Marney was a devout man who died in 1523, after building a turreted gatehouse which has been described as a masterpiece to rival Cardinal Wolsey's gatehouse at Hampton Court. His lordship's ghost is said to haunt at the top of the tower, slamming shut a door which is always kept bolted and barred.

Mother Marnes—Ye Olde Gatehouse, Highgate, London

Some called her Widow Marnes, some called her Mother. Either way she was murdered at the Gatehouse for her money, along with her cat, and haunts the old minstrels' gallery. She appears as a black-robed figure, which seldom manifests itself when children or animals are on the premises. One landlord who saw this ghost never really recovered from the shock and later gave up the tenancy on his doctor's advice.

George Marsh—Smithills Hall, Lancashire

The Reverend Marsh, a farmer before becoming a priest, held

Protestant views which so angered Mary Tudor that she had him 'examined' for heresy at Smithills Hall. As he was being escorted along the chapel passage, he protested his innocence and stamped his foot, calling on God to be a witness. Almost immediately a bloody footprint appeared on the flag-stone floor, where it can be seen to this day. Within days of that incident George Marsh was burned at the stake, leaving his ghost to haunt the chapel passage in white vestments, holding a book in one hand.

Elsie Marshall—Blackheath, London

Elsie Marshall, a girl of twenty, sailed for China in October 1892 to become a missionary with the Church of England Zenana Society. Before that she had spent fifteen years in Blackheath, where her father had moved from the Midlands to become Vicar of St John's Park. Little more than a year after joining her first mission school, Elsie was killed by Chinese bandits who massacred the entire settlement. Recently Elsie's ghost is thought to have returned to her old Blackheath home, now a branch library, where staff have experienced an invisible body brushing past in rooms and passageways, as well as turning on lights after closing hours.

Lady Margaret Massingberd—Gunby Hall, Lincolnshire

Lady Margaret's determination to marry the man she loved—a postillion-rider in her father's employ—ended in tragedy. Just as determined that his daughter should have nothing whatever to do with a man beneath her station, Sir William Massingberd, Squire of Gunby, took his twelve-bore and shot him dead as the couple were about to elope. The girl grieved herself into an early grave and, with her murdered lover, frequents a path near the eighteenth-century hall, known as the Ghosts' Walk.

Archdeacon Edmund Mervyn—and the seventeen ghosts of Bramshott, Hampshire

The Archdeacon, a non-conformist of Elizabethan vintage, is simply a 'front-man' for the seventeen-strong phantom population of Bramshott. He haunts his former home in the village, sharing it with another spectral resident, a White Lady whose identity is unknown.

Behind them, transparent shoulder to transparent shoulder are as follows.

Gamekeeper Adams, who knew the delights of the Royal Hampshire Forest of Woolmer in Queen Elizabeth's day, and sits outside his cottage savouring a clay of that new-fangled baccy, while along the lane a fair-haired shepherd boy is sometimes heard playing his pipe.

In the water-meadow, the shade of Mistress Elizabeth Butler walks where she drowned her unhappy self in 1745 and, near the church, a little girl in a poke bonnet is seen to walk through the churchyard wall and disappear.

A Quaker haunts the local manor house, a Grey Lady loiters close to where she plunged to her death down a well, and a pot-boy's phantom still lingers from the thirsty days of coaching.

A host of ghosts in Tudor dress have been seen *and* heard talking in subdued voices as they walk along one of Bramshott's leafy lanes, and, near a lodge-house in the village, the wraith of a woman is occasionally visible in the presence of children.

To put it at the top of the league table for The Most Haunted Village in England, Bramshott also boasts of a coach and horses which clatters by with regularity, a mounted cavalier, a murdered highwayman, a white calf which reduces to the size of a cat, a black pig which does nothing more than be its ghostly self, and yet another victim of drowning.

'Spider' Marshall—The Bear Inn, Stock, Essex

The most distinctive thing about Charlie Marshall was his sideways walk, which earned him the name 'Spider'. At the turn of the century, this pint-sized character was ostler at The Bear, where his favourite trick, to earn a pint, was to scramble up the huge chimney of the tap-room to the bacon loft and shoot down into the adjacent bar-parlour. At times when he was feeling cussed, he'd stay up there until he was smoked out. One Christmas Eve, full of beer and bravado, he would not budge from his sooty perch, so the locals kindled faggots and pushed them into the chimney. 'Spider', half asleep, suffocated, and, as far as is known, his old, blackened bones are still up there, while his ghost haunts the 400-year-old inn below. Every Christmas, a dozen men of Essex who form the exclusive Spider Club, gather to drink the health of this ghost.

Martha—Brede, Sussex

Martha is the ghost of a servant girl who was employed at Brede in Tudor times. As a punishment for stealing, her master hanged her from an ash tree which used to be in the dell behind the fourteenth-century house. A gate, near to where she died, is called Martha's Gate, and the awesome atmosphere around that spot was particularly evident, especially after dark, though a recent exorcism has done much to reduce it.

There is also the wraith of the benign Father John, a priest who used to live in Brede Chapel some hundreds of years ago.

Martyn's Ape—Athelhampton, Dorset

The Martyn family who lived at Athelhampton for four centuries, from the days of Henry III, kept apes as pets. The family crest was an ape and so is Athelhampton's ghost. The story goes that one of the Martyn daughters committed suicide in a tiny room reached by a concealed staircase, through a secret door. One of the apes which followed her through the secret door became imprisoned when the unhappy girl slammed the door shut; the ape slowly starved to death.

For generations now the ghost ape has not been seen, although other ghosts have. For instance, the Black Priest, and the shade of a cooper hammering in the cellar. In the Great Hall phantom swordsmen have been seen duelling until one is wounded. Then they vanish.

Bonnie May Marye—Askerton Castle, Cumbria

Bonnie May is known locally as the White Lady of Askerton,

where her ghostly white form is seen in the vicinity of the castle, a battlemented farmstead built by the Dacre family in early Tudor times. A century later, Bonnie May was murdered by a frustrated lover at a spot nearby called Yellow Coat Slack, and ever since has haunted over a wide area from Brampton to Bewcastle, once pursuing the Rector of Bewcastle, the Reverend Maughan, as he was riding home.

John (Topsy Turvy) Massey—Bilstone, Warwickshire

Early in life, John Massey was a wrestler and, because of his spectacular trick of hurling opponents backwards over his head, he earned the nickname Topsy Turvy. As well as great strength, he had a violent temper, as his second wife found out too late; he gave her a beating, from which she died after languishing for nearly two months. Massey was convicted for her murder and gibbeted on Red Hill, half a mile from Bilstone, on 30 March 1801. The gibbet is still there, and, some say, so is Topsy Turvy's ghost.

Mad Maude—Weston on the Green, Oxfordshire

Mad Maude was a young nun burned at the stake for her immoral behaviour, in the fifteenth century. Her ghost haunts the Weston Manor Hotel, which, five centuries ago, was a monastery, where the simple-minded Maude transgressed with the lustful brothers once too often and ended her days shrieking for mercy as the blazing faggots fried her feet.

Other hauntings at the Weston Manor are a phantom coach and horses seen at night careering through the courtyard of the old stables, and the ghost of a dairymaid found dying after what was thought to be a suicide leap from the tower.

Lady May—Park Lane East, Tipton, Staffordshire

Lady May was the seven-year-old daughter of a Leicestershire squire. Whenever her father had business in Tipton he took his little girl with him and put up at an inn called The Park, where Lady May had an attic room of her own. After an early morning riding excursion, she had a severe nose bleed which developed into a fatal haemorrhage. She died alone in her tiny bedroom, her father having to go out on a matter of urgency. That little Victorian melodrama has left an echo, in the attic of The Park, a presence which has dogs and humans alike fearful of going up to Lady May's room.

Old Charlie Miles—Frimley, Surrey

He wears a brown leather jacket and corduroy trousers, tied at the knee with string. A deer-stalker hat covers his grey hair and running near his feet is a small brown dog. That's the ghost of 'Old Charlie Miles', as everybody fondly knew him locally—walking his dog in the old Guildford Road, as he did most evenings before his sudden death in 1957. A retired lieutenant-colonel, he lived with his wife at Frimley Green, in a house they bought for their only son, an Army doctor, who was accidentally shot by a sentry in Singapore.

Johnnie Minney—Waresley, Huntingdon

An Australian woman, on a visit to England in 1965, stayed with friends at a 500-year-old farmhouse in the Huntingdon village of Waresley, where she was totally unknown. In the middle of her first night there, she awoke to see a small boy, pathetically thin and with pale, pinched cheeks, kneeling by her bed, crying for his mother. When she spoke the figure disappeared. Her inquiries during her stay revealed that what she had seen was the ghost of four-year-old Johnnie Minney, who died of meningitis in 1921, in that same room.

'Old Moses'—Prestbury, Gloucestershire

'Old Moses' is Prestbury's best identified ghost, a former racehorse trainer who lived at Walnut Cottage. Once a familiar figure at most Cheltenham race meetings, he is now no more than a ghostly shade of his former self, seen occasionally with one of his mares, in a converted stable near the Prestbury course.

Other wraiths reputed to haunt the village are the Black Abbot, seen in the High Street, St Mary's Church and the Priory; a galloping cavalier, said to be a Royalist despatch rider en route to Cheltenham with news of the battle of Worcester; a girl playing a spinet in the garden of Sundial Cottage, and the not-so-friendly phantom strangler of Cleve Corner.

Colonel Mulliner—Rainham, Essex

The Friendly Colonel, as this ghost is known locally, was the owner of Rainham Hall in Edwardian days. He became so fond of the place his wraith still lingers—in broad daylight—dressed in the fashionable gear of 1910—grey tweeds and a masher collar.

Irene Munro—Pevensey, Sussex

The body of Irene Munro, a young London typist murdered in 1920, was hidden on the shingle beach at Pevensey Bay where a blob of greenish light, resembling the traditional corpse-light, is sometimes seen.

This is within sight of the fourteenth-century Mint House, haunted by a young girl murdered there in 1586. Thomas Dight, the jealous lover who killed her, also killed one of her admirers by roasting him over an open fire.

N

Awd Nance—Burton Agnes Hall, nr Bridlington, Humberside

The Fawn Lady who haunts Burton Agnes Hall is endearingly called Awd Nance, though, in fact, it is the ghost of Anne Griffiths, whose skull is preserved here for posterity. Anne, youngest of three sisters who inherited the hall in late Elizabethan times, was the victim of a mugging within sight and sound of her home. Her dying wish was that her head should remain forever within the house which meant so much to her. As a precaution against it being removed and so causing 'diabolical disturbances and unearthly noises', the shrivelled relic is built into the wall of the great hall.

Nance—Claxton, North Yorkshire

This farmer's daughter from Sherriff Hutton left a ghost which frequents the roads of North Yorkshire, particularly a stretch of the A64 between Barton Hill and Claxton. She was engaged to a local lad named Tom Priestly, a stage-coach driver, but left him for a glib-talking stranger, who abandoned her when she gave birth to his child. Fortuitously it was Tom who found her, ill and destitute, beside the road at Claxton. Nance died in Tom's arms that same night, leaving him with her child to care for and a whispered promise that her spirit would always range the roads around York, watching over him and his kin. Until the turn of last century, the name of Nance was known to most innkeepers between York and Teesside, and to most of the men in the driving seat as far north as the Tweed. There are lorry drivers who claim to have seen the ghost of Nance on the Yorkshire roads of today, usually when the weather is foul.

The Naseby Phenomenon—Northamptonshire

The spectral re-enactment of the great Civil War battle fought at Naseby seems to have faded with time. For almost a hundred years after the Royalists were routed by Cromwell, in 1645, succeeding generations of village folk from miles around, gathered on the anniversary of the bloody event to see it all 'played back' in the sky. By all reports this aerial manifestation, known as the Naseby Phenomenon, was complete in every detail; not only did the watchers *see* the armies in action, they also heard the din of battle, even the groans of the injured. A phantom army was also seen marching across Cumbria's Souter Fell, on Midsummer-eve, 1745.

Georgiana Naylor—Hurstmonceaux Castle, Sussex

Georgiana Naylor has been described as 'a beautiful eccentric' who resided at Hurstmonceaux in the closing years of the eighteenth century. She was interested in the occult and wore a white cloak decorated with mystic symbols. Daily she rode on a white ass to drink in the park from an enchanted spring, a tame white doe running by her side. The day after stray dogs chased the doe, and ripped it to pieces, she left Hurstmonceaux, returning only after her death, in 1806, as a ghost riding a spectral white ass.

Grace Naylor—Hurstmonceaux Castle, Sussex

The daughter of George Naylor, who bought the castle in 1708, haunts this place in which she died on the eve of her twenty-first birthday. She was starved to death in the half-ruined east wing of the castle, though for what reason it has never been established. It was rumoured her governess was paid to murder her by starvation, to deny her the fortune she should have inherited on coming of age in 1727. Occasionally, her gaunt figure has been seen in the corridors, but more frequently her ghost is heard—quietly sobbing.

Geoffrey Netherwood—Ilford Fire Station, Essex

Geoffrey Netherwood was a fireman in Victorian London, stationed at Ilford, at the old Broadway fire station. Between calls, he lovingly polished his tunic brasses, as well as keeping the horses and harness in immaculate readiness. When he died, his gleaming brass helmet rested on the coffin, as colleagues carried him to his grave. However, Fireman Netherwood did not rest for long. His spectral figure, in old fashioned helmet and high-buttoned tunic, was seen many times in the old Broadway station. More recently it has been seen at Ilford's new fire depot in Romford Road.

Reverend Percy Newall—West Borough, Dorset

Dressed in clerical black, with a Bible under one arm, this phantom figure is reputed to be the Reverend Newall who, between 1843 and 1875, lived in West Borough at King's House, though in those days it was known as Garden House. It is next door to Dickens's

House, wherein the reverend gentleman has been seen emerging from the wall at a spot where there was once a doorway, which he is heard opening at six o'clock in the morning.

Polly Nicholls—Durward Street, London

Polly's only claim to fame was being Jack the Ripper's first victim. She was a forty-two-year-old prostitute who died in the gutter of Durward Street, Whitechapel, on 31 August 1888, her throat and abdomen slashed. Her ghost spares us that grisly sight, though what has been witnessed is 'a huddled figure, like that of a woman, emitting from all over it a ghostly light, frequently to be seen lying in the gutter.'

Ghostly harrowing groans and screams heard in nearby Hanbury Street, Spitalfields, were reputedly from another of the Ripper's prostitute victims, forty-seven-year-old Annie Chapman.

Thomas Nicholson—Beacon Edge Road, Penrith, Cumbria

Tom Nicholson's mouldering bones lie in a shallow grave close by the stone which marks the spot where the gibbet once stood at the top of Beacon Edge Road. For two bleak winters Nicholson's body swung from that gibbet arm, after he had been condemned for robbing and murdering his godfather, a butcher from Langwathby, in August 1767. But, even today, there are villagers of nearby Eden Hall, who say Nicholson's ghostly body still swings on Gibbet Hill on stormy nights—a weather-bleached skeleton rattling eerily at the end of a rotting gallows.

Ivor Novello—Palace Theatre, London

Among theatre people it is believed that the ghost of Ivor Novello, actor, dramatist and composer, haunts the dress circle of the Palace Theatre, in London's Cambridge Circus. But there are those who say that Novello would haunt nowhere but the Adelphi, since it was there he had one of his greatest successes with his musical *The Dancing Years*. He was entrenched in the star dressing room for most of the war years, and there are actors and actresses who are convinced the phantom Novello is responsible for the many uncanny incidents which are otherwise inexplicable.

O

Richard Oastler—Bolling Hall, Bradford, West Yorkshire

Oastler, nineteenth-century campaigner for factory reform, and a believer in an after-life, was a frequent caller at Bolling at the time the Walker family lived there. He once told the Walker's son that if he (the son) did not believe in life after death, he (Oastler) would return as a ghost. That he did, on 22 August 1861, the same day as he died.

Another haunting at Bolling Hall, from the time when the Royalist Duke of Newcastle used it as his headquarters, has gone down in history. Everybody in this Parliamentary stronghold was to be slaughtered at dawn on the Duke's orders and no doubt would have been, had the Duke not had a restless night, during which he saw a female figure in white at his bedside, wringing her hands and pleading 'Pity, Poor Bradford'. After seeing it three times he rescinded the previous day's order.

Kate Oatway—Chambercome, Devon

Kate Oatway was starved to death and walled-up in the secret room of Chambercombe Manor, where her cobweb-covered skeleton remained for 150 years. This teenage daughter of William Oatway, a notorious wrecker living at Chambercome in the seventeenth century, was forgotten by the world until 1865, when a farmer stumbled on the grisly remains on a four-poster bed behind rotting curtains. It is assumed to be her ghost which haunts the manor, walking in the corridors and in the cobbled courtyard. But why Kate had to die so cruelly remains a mystery. Was it because she threatened to reveal her father's wrecking activities that William Oatway decided on that sadistic method of keeping her quiet?

Jack O'Cassiobury—near Watford, Hertfordshire

Jack O'Cassiobury was a negro slave in eighteenth-century England. He was given his name by his wealthy woman owner whose property skirted the Grand Union Canal where it passes through Cassiobury Park, above Watford. Because of his great strength and agility, and because she was opposed to the waterway, she employed him to harass the coal barges as they passed through Ironbridge Lock. His Tarzan-like tactics resulted in daily chaos and, ultimately, in Jack's death. Knocked senseless into the lock by an irate bargee, he was left to drown. Which is why many boatmen on the Grand Union, even today, shun Ironbridge Lock after dark, to avoid encountering Jack's still agile ghost.

Another of Cassiobury's ghosts is that of Lord Capel, a Roundhead who became a Royalist during the Civil War. He puts in an appearance on the anniversary of his execution, 9 March 1649.

Peg O'Nell—Ribblesdale, Lancashire

A statue of St Margaret gave this ghost its name. Today, it stands headless and overgrown in a Ribbleside meadow near Waddow Hall, watching over a long disused well and the nearby stepping stones across the river. Many a long-ago traveller whispered a prayer to Saint-Peg-of-the-Well for a safe crossing. First reports of a ghost followed a winter tragedy; a servant from the Hall, ordered to fetch water, lost her way in deep snow and fell into the ice-covered Ribble. Superstitious local folk quickly dubbed her ghost Peg O' The Well, blaming her for any subsequent local disaster.

The Old Maids of Llangollen—North Wales

According to tradition, only men can see the 'Old Maids of Llangollen' who are reputed to walk at Plas Newydd every Christmas Eve. These two eighteenth-century Irish eccentrics,

Lady Eleanor Butler and Miss Sarah Ponsonby, who always dressed as men, are seen, but once a year, drifting around their old home in their best male attire.

The ruins of an old fisherman's cottage beside the River Dee at Llangollen are haunted by the apparition of a young woman.

Dickey O'Tunstead—Tunstead Milton, Derbyshire

Dickey is 'the screaming skull' of Derbyshire, resident at Tunstead Farm, having survived being twice buried as well as thrown into both river and reservoir. Whenever it has been discarded trouble has followed, though when kept in its niche, it seems to protect the house, once being instrumental in catching an intruder. Dickie's Bridge is still there to prove the skull's biggest supernatural success—causing the railway to be routed round the farm instead of across it. The ghostly skull is thought to come from the shoulders of Ned Dickson who returned from the Huguenot wars, only to be murdered by his cousin who had taken over his farm. A rival legend claims the skull is female, belonging to a co-heiress who was murdered, leaving a ghost which has been seen in the house from time to time.

Donna Leonora Oviedo—Thorpe Hall, Lincolnshire

Donna Leonora is the Green Lady of Louth, considered one of the most beautiful ghosts in Britain. She was among prisoners taken by Sir John Bolles at the fall of Cadiz, in 1596. After becoming her lover, as well as her gaoler, Sir John returned to England without her, and a despairing Leonora stabbed herself to death. Her ghost, gowned in shimmering green as she was the day they first met, pursued Sir John to his Lincolnshire home and haunted him to his grave. Within recent years, she caused a cyclist to fall off his machine and a local vicar to become dumbfounded, after she walked bone-dry in front of his car in a rain storm.

P

Brother Pacificus—Ranworth, Norfolk

Brother Pacificus, a monk from St Benet's Abbey, every day at dawn, rowed himself and his dog across Ranworth Broad, to his place of work. It is on record that, in the 1530s, he was restoring the rood-screen in Ranworth Church as a labour of love. One summer evening, the restoration almost complete, the monk rowed back to find the Abbey burned and pillaged and many of his brothers dead at the hand of the King's men. For years after, he lived, hermit-like, in the ruins and eventually died there. Knowing of his devotion to Ranworth Church, the villagers buried him in the churchyard on the far side of the Broad, which accounts for the small boat that is sometimes seen in the dawn light, rowed by a monk in a black habit with a little dog sitting in the bow.

Paddy—Didsbury, Greater Manchester

Paddy is a small black phantom dog seen in the garden of an old house at the junction of Spath Road and Holme Road, Didsbury. He was seen by a policeman of the Manchester City force, on a clear moonlight night in 1957. He walked across the lawn and was lost to sight behind a large tree, yet, when the policeman looked behind the tree, the dog was nowhere to be seen. Investigating the mystery in daylight, the constable found a small moss-covered stone at the base of the tree where the dog disappeared. On it the words: 'Paddy. Died September 2nd, 1913'.

Madam Papillon—Lubenham, Leicestershire

The name of Madam Papillon is still remembered in the countryside around Lubenham. For years after she was murdered, until

Papillon Hall was demolished, a dainty pair of her French-made shoes was exhibited in a recess in the panelled walls. If that didn't keep the memories alive, her ghost certainly did, careering a four-in-hand along the main road leading to the village. And, in recent years, there's been evidence that Madam's ghost is still at large, seen usually in the very early hours, near the village inn.

Sir Hubert Parry—Rustington, Sussex

Sir Hubert, probably as well remembered for 'Jerusalem' as for any of his concertos and symphonies, lived in Rustington from 1879. He personally supervised the building of Knightscroft House, where he lived until he died in 1918. When his ghost was seen to walk through a wall, before the very eyes of the new owner, his expression was described as 'kindly', which is how the people of Rustington thought of him, particularly the forty-six men who worked on Knightscroft; it is noted they were rewarded with 'a feast which included plenty of liquid refreshment, followed by games'.

John Paslew—Whalley Abbey, Lancashire

There is photographic evidence of this ghost, taken in 1966 by a photographer from the *Clitheroe Advertiser*. The 'tall, dark shadow' pictured hurrying along a lane in the vicinity of Whalley Abbey, is believed to be the ghost of John Paslew, last Abbot of Whalley, sent to the gallows in 1537 for his part in the Pilgrimage of Grace.

Elizabeth Pateman—Steeple Morden, Cambridge

This nineteen-year-old servant girl was overheard whispering to her lover that she had a secret to tell him. Her eavesdropping master thought only that she was meaning the killing of the pedlar who had called and whose body he had dumped in the well. To be sure of her silence and of his own skin, he killed her too. It all happened in 1750, at Moco Farm, now a haunted ruin, where Elizabeth's ghost cries out in pain and terror as she did when done to death with peahook, knife and coulter.

Lady Joan Pelham—Pevensey Castle, Sussex

Lady Pelham defended Pevensey Castle for the red rose of Lancaster, against an army of Surrey, Kent and Sussex men, in 1399. She withstood a long seige with dwindling supplies, while her husband, Sir John, was away in Pontefract fighting for the Yorkists. A figure 'dressed in peculiar clothes' has been seen standing on the castle walls as if surveying the scene below, as no doubt Lady Pelham did many times during that grim battle. There are those who doubt the ghost is that of the gallant Lady Pelham, suggesting a more likely supernatural resident to be Queen Joan of Navarre, wife of Henry IV, a prisoner in Pevensey for nine years.

Kate Penfound—Penfound Manor, Cornwall

Kate Penfound, whose family were Royalists to the marrow, loved a Roundhead, John Trebarfoot, son of a near neighbour. Had it not been for the Civil War, Kate and John would have married, but Kate's father, Arthur Penfound, forbade it, leaving the young couple no option but to elope. Tragically Arthur Penfound stumbled upon them as they tried to slip away from Penfound Manor on the night of 26 April, and shot them both in the courtyard, below Kate's bedroom window. Not only does Kate's ghost walk down the Stuart staircase and across the Great Hall to disappear on the main street, but her father's ghost has also been seen.

Mrs Sibell Penn—Hampton Court Palace, Middlesex

The spectre of Mrs Sibell Penn, foster mother to Jane Seymour's sickly child who, aged ten, became Edward VI, has been seen at Hampton Court, although more frequently she is heard, treadling away at her spinning wheel. The fretful Royal infant was often lulled to sleep by the rhythmic whirr, accompanied by Mrs Penn's voice. After her death from smallpox in 1568, her ghost made its presence known to the family occupying her old apartments. They complained of someone spinning and talking behind a wall where there was no known room. When workmen broke through the wall, a sealed room was revealed and in it a well used spinning wheel and other feminine oddments.

Captain Henry Penruddock—West Lavington, Wiltshire

The Penruddocks were King's men, whose name is best remembered by Colonel John Penruddock's successful, though short-lived, storming of Salisbury, ending in the Colonel's execution. Twelve years earlier, in 1643, Captain Henry fought at Roundway to the north of Devizes, after which he'd ridden hard to West Lavington for refuge at the home of the Becketts. There he fell into a chair and was soundly asleep when Parliamentary soldiers came searching. One of Cromwell's troopers entered the house and shot him dead as he slept. His name is recalled by appearances of his slumbering ghost, less frequent since the house was partly rebuilt in 1903.

Sir Josceline Percy—Beverley, Humberside

The ghost of Sir Josceline youngest son of the 4th Earl of Northumberland has been abroad on the streets of Beverley since a September day in 1532. But only on wild and stormy nights is he seen, driving a phantom coach pulled by four black horses, usually described as headless, while inside the swaying vehicle sits a skeleton, a grisly spectacle which foretells trouble, even death, for those who see it. It's not to be wondered that Sir Josceline cannot rest quietly in his grave, after changing his will in favour of three servants who promptly poisoned him and made off with his wealth to neighbouring Walton Hall, the home of Sir Thomas Waterton.

Peter the Great—King's Arms Royal Hotel, Godalming, Surrey

Tsar Peter the Great of Russia seems to have left his ghostly mark on the King's Arms after staying there in 1698. He and his party, described by John Evelyn, the seventeenth-century diarist, as 'a right nasty lot', were en route from Portsmouth. It is suggested that the ghost, which manifests itself by kicking off a pair of heavy boots between 1 and 2 am, is that of the Tsar, though it is just as likely to be Nelson or Henry VIII disposing of their buckled shoes; both slept here.

The Phantom of the A23—Pyecombe, Sussex

Those who have seen the ghost of the Brighton Road usually describe it as a young blonde woman dressed in a pale-coloured mackintosh. She appears to haunt an area of the A23 about ten miles north of Brighton. In the 1960s a motorist, driving south from Crawley, reported seeing a figure in a white mackintosh run across the road to the central reservation and disappear. In 1972 there were eye-witness accounts of a limping blonde girl seen north of Pyecombe and said to be the ghost of a young girl hitch-hiker killed in a motor-cycle accident. Other motorists claim to have seen a ghost in cricketing clothes, as well as a tall slender woman in a cape with a hood, and at her side the figure of a child, similarly dressed.

The Phantom Chicken of Highgate—Pond Square, London

Kneeling in a blizzard by the duck pond, on top of Highgate Hill, cramming frozen snow into the carcass of a freshly plucked chicken, was too much for the frail sixty-year-old Sir Francis Bacon. This attempt, in 1626, to test his theory about refrigeration led to his death from bronchitis. However, it is not his spectre which has for many years since haunted Pond Square in consequence, but the ghost of a chicken, described as 'featherless, flapping its wing stubs and squawking, eventually disappearing into a brick wall'.

The Phantom Fiddle—Poole, Dorset

This instrument, made in 1889, belonged originally to a violinist in the orchestra on board the ill-fated liner *Titanic*. As the ship was sinking in the North Atlantic, passengers sang 'Nearer my God to thee', with the violinist accompanying them. Though he survived the disaster, he never played again and sold the violin to a Mr Calver for £20.

A Poole auctioneer, Mr Fred Calver, who inherited the instrument from his father, put it up for auction in 1966. But he got no bids, because his father's ghost had returned a number of times to play it, since his death the year before.

The Phantom Funeral—of Wootton Street, Bedworth, Warwickshire

In the years between the world wars, there were reports from the Midlands town of Bedworth of a ghostly funeral procession. It was usually encountered early on winter mornings while it was still dark. Those who saw it reported that they became aware of some kind of procession of shadowy horse-drawn carriages as they entered the lower end of Wootton Street. It was obviously a funeral cortege of the Edwardian era, but it seemed impossible to overtake it, no matter how fast one walked. When the end of the street was reached the whole thing vanished.

The Phantom General—Cambridge Gardens, London

This ghost has nothing to do with the army. It is a phantom General Omnibus on the No 7 route of the 1930s. It has not been seen of late, but there was a time when it ran a 'regular' service. Those who lived in Cambridge Gardens were awakened by the noise of the ghost bus racing by, all lit up but without a driver or conductor. On reaching the junction of Cambridge Gardens and St Marks Road, the bus dissolved into thin air. Not until a motorist was killed in 1934, after swerving to avoid the phantom General, was this phenomenon taken seriously.

The Phantom Monks of St Dunstan's—East Acton, London

Press publicity has resulted in this ghostly phenomena becoming as well known in America as in Britain. Since the 1930s, there have been regular reports of phantom monks walking in procession in St Dunstan's Church. They are reckoned to be a spectral flashback to the time of Henry I, when a monastic settlement was established in the vicinity by friars who followed Rahere, the monk who founded St Bartholomew the Great. A vicar of St Dunstan's, a man in his fifties, and once an army chaplain, described the phenomena in these words: 'About a dozen monks can be seen on most evenings walking in procession up the centre aisle and into the chancel. They wear golden brown habits and are hooded. Another monk in eucharistic vestments occasionally celebrates Mass in the memorial chapel.'

The Phantom Nurse—St Thomas's Hospital, London

'One of the most remarkable examples of a ghost ever recorded', says Bill Neech, former editor of *Psychic News*, is the figure of a distraught nurse, seen on the top floor of Block 8 of old St Thomas' Hospital. Many of the doctors, nurses and administrative staff have seen the phantom figure in a Crimea grey uniform, aged about thirty-five, and so lifelike that Dr T. Anwyl-Davies, a hospital physician, raised his hat and wished her 'Good morning.' After telling his experience to the assistant matron, he heard for the first time about the apparition of a nurse of the 1880s who leapt to her death from the balcony of Block 8, following a violent quarrel with a martinet sister.

The Phantom Persian—All Hallows by the Tower, London

A ghost cat, a white Persian, haunted the porch-room and organ loft of All Hallows, until church and ghost were destroyed in the German blitz on London. The cat was the pet of Miss Liscette Rist, woman organist at the church, 1840–80, whose regard for animals caused her to scatter gravel for the horses using the steep, icy roads near the Tower. When the white Persian died, it is said Miss Rist was refused permission for it to be buried in consecrated ground, so surreptitiously buried it herself. The ghostly animal was seen several times before World War I, and between the wars, but has not been reported since the rebuilding of All Hallows.

The Phantom Spitfire—Biggin Hill, Kent

A lone Spitfire is said to materialise and scream low over the

Battle of Britain airfield at Biggin Hill. Though it is not always visible as it roars in to land, witnesses report the noise is unmistakably that of a war time fighter. There have been times, say some, when the long-dead RAF pilot signals his return from the sortie with a low victory roll.

At Hawkinge, near Folkestone, the vibrant throb of a flying bomb is sometimes heard in the empty sky—thirty or more years after the German VI offensive ceased.

Old Doctor Phene—Glebe Place, Chelsea, London

Dr Phene was one of the characters of old Chelsea. He lived in Glebe Place in a big house with a large garden which, when the demolition men moved in after old Doctor Phene's death, gave up its secrets. First they unearthed a ruined church, then the bones of a horse which the Doctor had been fanatically fond of, it having once saved his life. He buried it within sight of his study window and, since his death, many have claimed seeing the ghost of the old doctor astride his horse, in the vicinity of Oakley Street and Upper Cheyne Row.

Mademoiselle Pinard—Meopham, Kent

Privateer Dick Bennett returned from the war in France with his newly acquired mistress, Mademoiselle Pinard. He took her to Steel's Lane, Meopham, to live with the wife he had left behind when he went off to fight Napolean's army. But Bennett's wife made life intolerable for her husband's new girl friend, so much so that Mademoiselle Pinard went out of her mind. She dressed herself in her best gown of orange-coloured silk, then hanged herself. Her unhappy ghost, the Orange Girl of Meopham, haunts Steel's Lane near the old village green, with three other ghosts for company—a nineteenth-century miller named Bennett; a servant girl at Dean Manor, and a headless man, seen to walk from the inn to the church.

The Plate-layer—Tulse Hill, London

A plate-layer, killed by an electric train as he walked along the track, is said to haunt Tulse Hill station. A comparatively modern ghost this, stemming from the early 1920s, about the time electric trains were being introduced to south London. The noise of a gale force wind, and of an approaching steam engine, blotted out the sound of the electric train, which ran him down from behind. In pre-Beeching days, night duty staff at Tulse Hill many times talked of hearing the heavy, deliberate footsteps of the plate-layer's ghost, stamping along No 1 platform and onto the track.

Lady Plumley—Locking, Somerset

This tragic noblewoman stood by helplessly while her husband, Sir John Plumley, Lord of the Manor of Locking, was executed by the King's troopers within sight of the home he had left to fight for Monmouth at Sedgemoor. Had his favourite dog not been so pleased at its master's return, he might have been able to escape, but furious barking brought the pursuing soldiers running and he was dragged to an elm tree and hanged. Lady Plumley, overwhelmed with horror, snatched up the dog and threw herself and the animal down a well. The ghost of her ladyship with a phantom dog in her arms walks in the garden, fading away at the edge of the long disused well.

Lady Margaret de Pomeroy—Berry Pomeroy Castle, Devon

Beware the ghost of Lady Margaret; she may lure you to your death if you heed her beckoning finger. She was one of two sisters who faced a dilemma of jealousy, both having fallen in love with the same man. Lady Eleanor de Pomeroy, mistress of the castle, solved the problem by 'sentencing' her pretty younger sister to solitary confinement in a dungeon beneath one of the towers, where she slowly starved to death. The ghost of Lady Margaret, her once lovely face grotesquely withered, walks the castle ramparts gesturing to those who see her to join her in her dungeon tomb.

Another ghost seen within the castle grounds has been dubbed 'The Blue Lady', because of her long, blue gown. Legend has it that she is searching for her baby, born of an incestuous relationship with her father, another of the Pomeroy family.

Alexander Pope—Twickenham, Middlesex

Statesmen, men of letters, wits and beauties were all ready to pay homage to Pope as the greatest poet of his time. He and his mother entertained them at the villa in Twickenham to which they moved after his father's death in 1718. When Pope died, in 1744, he was buried in the riverside churchyard of St Mary's, where the ghost of the crippled poet is now less frequently seen, but still heard, dragging his deformed leg. The haunting seems to date from 1830, when Pope's skull was stolen from his coffin to become the showpiece of the private collection of phrenologist Johann Spurzheim.

The Prehistoric Man—Bottlebush Down, Dorset

A prehistoric horseman of the Bronze Age has been seen cantering across open downland between Cranborne and Sixpenny Handley, in Dorset. A Fellow of the Royal Society of Archaeologists encountered this most ancient of ghosts one evening as he drove home to Fovant. He could see that it was no ordinary horseman, for he had bare legs, and wore a long, loose cloak, and he used neither bridle nor stirrups. In his right hand he brandished what looked like a stone axe. For about a hundred yards he pounded along at the side of the car, then vanished by an ancient burial mound.

Thomas Pryde—Bradbourne House, Kent

On the morning of 30 January 1649, Thomas Pryde, one of those who put his ignoble signature to King Charles's death warrant, rode out to Bradbourne House, in Kent, to try to avoid his conscience as the axe fell. Seemingly his troubled ghost, a cloaked figure on a great grey horse, still makes the dramatic ride, galloping like a whirlwind through Barming Woods and over the heath.

Sir Robert Pye—Faringdon, Berkshire

The headless ghost, seen at dusk by the north wall of All Saints Church, Faringdon, is thought to be Sir Robert Pye. As a Roundhead, he had the unpleasant duty of attacking his own home, Wadley Hall, defended by his father in the name of the King. The fact that this ghost is headless and that Sir Robert died of old age in 1701, suggests a mistaken identity; some say the spectre is one of the Unton family, beheaded during the Civil War.

R

Radiant Boy—Corby Castle, Cumbria

One of the most spectacular hauntings of the nineteenth century was the luminous figure of an unidentified boy, first seen at Corby in 1803 by the Rector of Greystoke. It has not been witnessed since December 1834. Legend has it that anyone seeing the spectre of a radiant boy would rise to fame and die violently, yet the Greystoke clergyman died peacefully of nothing more violent than old age. Not so Lord Castlereagh; he saw the boy in Ireland when an obscure army captain, rose to political fame and committed suicide in 1822.

Rahere—St Bartholomew the Great, London

Rahere was both a monk and a minstrel at the Court of Henry I. He built an Augustinian priory at Smithfield in 1123, parts of which still stand as the church of St Bartholomew the Great. It houses the tomb of Rahere and his ghost, seen on many occasions and by a number of different people, including several clergymen and church workers.

It has been reported that the ghost of the eighteenth-century painter, William Hogarth, his beaver hat at a jaunty angle, lingers in St Batholomews, the church in which he was baptized.

Sir Walter Raleigh—Beddington, Surrey

The great Raleigh mystery—where was he buried after his execution in 1618—may never be resolved. His embalmed head, which Lady Raleigh carried everywhere in a leather handbag, is interred at West Horsely, while St Margaret's, Westminster, claims the body, though Sir Walter's wife wrote to her brother, Nicholas Carew: '... let me bury the worthy body of my noble husband... in your church at Beddington...'. Perhaps, say some, his body lies in Westminster and his heart, alone, in the Carew vault at Beddington. Unfortunately, that cannot be searched because, in the 1880s, it was filled with concrete. Such desecration may be the reason Sir Walter haunts at Beddington in the vicinity of old Carew House, where he so often walked with Queen Elizabeth. He is said to haunt also at Sherborne Castle, where he is seen strolling in the grounds, or sitting under the tree which bears his name.

George Ransley—The Walnut Tree, Aldington, Kent

Among the smuggling fraternity, George Ransley was 'a real gentleman'. He commanded 'the Blues', a ruthless gang of Kentish smugglers, based on Aldington, where they used The Walnut Tree as their headquarters. From 1821–26, Ransley and 'the Blues' were the terror of the Romney Marshes, yet he was eventually taken in his bed, deported to Australia, and died a prosperous farmer. Behind him he left a ghost, thought to be one of the two which haunt The Walnut Tree. Legend has it that his spectral companion is one of his gang killed in a quarrel, whose body was dumped in the old well at the side of the pub.

The Rapist—Sandford Orcas, Dorset

It is claimed that the Manor at Sandford Orcas is haunted by fourteen ghosts, one of which is a tall, depraved footman who appears only in the presence of virgins. He is thought to have raped a number of the serving-maids and revisits the scene of one of his more brutal seductions.

Among the other supernatural tenants is a farmer who hanged himself in the gatehouse early in the 1700s. He appeared in the background of a family group photograph taken on the lawn, wearing a bowler hat and a white smock.

Margaret Reay—Admiralty House, London

This is the ghost Whitehall is loath to talk about. If you ask the Ministry of Works and Public Buildings about the haunting of the first floor flat in Admiralty House, the answer you will get is, 'Nothing more than noises in the water pipes, old boy'. But the ghostly young woman who appears from time to time, in what was Sir Winston Churchill's bedroom when he was First Sea Lord, is said to look remarkably like Margaret Reay, whose portrait hangs in Admiralty House. She was mistress of the Earl of Sandwich, shot dead by a jealous lover on the night of 7 April 1779, as she was leaving Covent Garden Theatre.

The Redhead—'Three Cocks', Brecon

A Green Lady with long red hair, who looks sad and sorry for herself, haunts the upper Wye Valley at the Three Cocks. The inn by that name had its beginnings as an isolated farmhouse, part of the Gwernyfed estate, sporting the three cockerels emblem of Einion Sais, the Welsh prince. Here Charles I lay low after being routed at Chester and, inevitably, the King's stay has been romantically linked with the Green Lady. But that is unlikely, though her habit of invariably materialising in Room 5, a room usually kept for men alone, suggests she may be looking for a lost lover.

Sir Henry Rich, First Earl of Holland—Holland House, London

Cromwell ordered this Royalist Earl to be executed in 1649. He went to his death at Palace Yard, Westminster, wearing a white satin waistcoat and a silver-trimmed white satin cap. He tipped the axeman £10, asking him to be careful of his clothes, and not to take the cap from his head after execution. The Earl's headless ghost still walks the grounds of Holland House, and, before the old place was almost totally destroyed by bombing in World War II, he also haunted the Gilt Room.

Hugh Ripley—Ripon, North Yorkshire

Hugh Ripley, seventeenth-century merchant of Ripon, was the city's last wakeman and its first mayor. His house in the market place—still called the Wakeman's House—is haunted by his ghost, seen looking from the small window at the top of the building if the evening ceremony of blowing the wakeman's horn is not performed properly. At the 1923 ceremony to mark the preservation of Hugh Ripley's house as a historic building, a vast crowd in the market place claimed to see the face at the window, but were divided as to whether it watched with disapproval or satisfaction.

Amy Robsart—Cornbury Park, Oxfordshire

Amy Robsart broke her neck falling down stairs in Cumnor Place on 8 September 1560. That her fall was probably arranged by her husband, Robert Dudley, so that he might marry Queen Elizabeth, has always been suspected. At the time gossip grew with the news that Amy's ghost had been seen on the fatal staircase, where she continued to haunt until the house was demolished in 1810. Even that did not stop her haunting the park and surviving an exorcism by twelve parsons from Oxford. It is said she still haunts Cornbury Park in Oxfordshire, where her husband died suddenly in 1588, after Amy's ghost appeared to him and warned him he was soon to die.

Lady Rokeby—Rokeby Park, Greta Bridge, Durham

Locally this ghost is known as the Mortham Dobby, a white lady who haunts the woods near Mortham's Tower, the fifteenth-century home of the Rokebys, one of whom stabbed his wife to death in a frenzy of jealousy. Recent stories in the *Northern Echo* suggest that the ghost is still to be seen, as are the bloodstains on the steps leading from the murder spot in the glen, below the old border pele tower.

Rosata—Chicksands Priory, Bedfordshire

American servicemen on the USAF base at Chicksands Priory call her The Wayward Nun. They are introduced to her in a document headed 'Illicit love affair', telling of Rosata's downfall 800 years ago, when canons and nuns of the Gilbertine Order occupied the priory. Rosata became pregnant as a result of a passionate association with one of the canons, for which indiscretion both paid with their lives; he was beheaded while she was walled up alive. RAF personnel at Chicksands, during World War II, claimed to have seen her ghost several times, corroborating the legend that Rosata walks the priory looking for the amorous canon on the 17th of each month.

Donald Ross—White Hart Inn, Chalfont St Peter, Buckinghamshire

Donald Ross, a nineteenth-century landlord of this pub, was seventy when he died and, almost to his last breath, he played the fiddle in the black-beamed bar, to keep his customers happy. Even now, a hundred years on, his ghost is still making music in the fourteenth-century inn, though it's usually long after closing time when the performance begins.

Christopher Round—Christ's College, Cambridge

The tall, black-clad, elderly figure of Christopher Round haunts the Fellows' Garden of Christ's College, walking with slow, ponderous steps, his hands clasped at his back, his head down. He always paces close to the mulberry tree planted by Milton, a ghost full of remorse for murdering another Fellow.

Christ's is also ghosted by a former don, a tall young man in a grey suit, usually seen in the second court of the college, as well as in adjacent lanes.

King William Rufus—New Forest, Hampshire

William Rufus died in the New Forest, killed by an arrow while hunting in the summer of 1100. The Rufus Stone marks the spot where a charcoal burner found the body, loaded it onto his cart and took it to Winchester. Red William's spectre haunts the glade of knotted thorn trees, called Castle Malwood, where he had a hunting lodge. He haunts also the 24-mile stretch of road by which the collier's cart carried his body to an unceremonious burial.

Prince Rupert—Edgehill, Warwickshire

Rupert of Bavaria, nephew of King Charles I, who, at twenty-two, led the Royalist cavalry into action in most of the major battles of the Civil War, haunts at Edgehill. He has been seen astride his white horse, holding aloft a staff as he charges with the same verve and dash as he did that historic day in 1642.

Edgehill, like many of the old battlefields, has a whole army of ghosts, soldiers of the King fighting those of Cromwell, in a spectral battle. It has been seen many times, since a few months after the original battle raged.

Ghost of Runway 1—Heathrow, London

Over the years many people have reported seeing a bowler-hatted ghost on Runway 1, at London's Heathrow Airport. A medium of the Spiritualist Association, visiting Heathrow, described the figure as 'ex-Guards' in his late forties, about 6ft tall, who appears to be searching for something. The description tallies with that of a bowler-hatted man encountered by rescue-workers, concerned about his lost brief case immediately after the crash of a DC3 aircraft at the airport on 2 March 1948. Twenty-two passengers, most of them businessmen, died when it burst into flames on the Heathrow runway.

S

Lady Scamler—Wolterton, Norfolk

Lady Scamler's ghost—the White Lady of Wolterton—spends most of her time searching for her tombstone. It is reputed that, after the Scamlers gave up Wolterton to the Lords Orford, many of the old family tombs in the church were destroyed, an act of sacrilege which caused the White Lady to go ahaunting, wandering the ruined church and graveyard seeking her resting place. The same White Lady is said to appear whenever a calamity is about to threaten the family.

Dame Dorothy Selby—Ightham Mote, Kent

Quite unintentionally, Dame Dorothy changed the course of English history—and died for it. It was she who sent an anonymous letter to her cousin, Lord Monteagle, imploring him to avoid Parliament on 5 November 1605. That tip-off brought a swift end to the Gunpowder Plot and slow death to Dame Dorothy who, it is generally supposed, was seized by friends of the plotters and bricked up in the tower of Ightham Mote. A woman's skeleton, discovered in a sealed cupboard at Ightham in 1872, was believed to be hers, and accounts for the intense and persistent coldness that pervades the adjoining tower bedroom.

Sellis—The Royal Valet—St James' Palace, London

Sellis, the Italian valet to Ernest Augustus, Duke of Cumberland, fifth son of George III, died a horrible death. He was found propped up in bed, his throat cut, his lower jaw hanging open in a macabre grin. This is just as his ghost is occasionally seen today, a gruesome flashback to the night of 31 May 1810, when the Duke returned from the opera to his St James' Palace apartments. At the inquest, the Duke said Sellis attacked him, but failed to kill him, so committed suicide. The gossips said differently, that the Duke having seduced his valet's daughter, murdered Sellis to put a stop to his blackmail.

The Severed Arm of Capesthorne Hall, Cheshire

Sir Bromley Davenport is the down-to-earth squire of Capesthorne Hall, near Macclesfield, where he has the company of 'a grey lady' and 'a number of spectre-like figures'. They have been vouched for time and again by several of his parliamentary friends, who have encountered one or other of them while overnighting in the mansion. His son's experience, in 1958, was perhaps the most unnerving. He woke to see an arm with nothing attached to it, groping towards the window near his bed. Since that night the bedroom has been known as 'the room with the severed arm'.

Lady Jane Seymour—Hampton Court Palace, Middlesex

Even before the unfortunate Anne Boleyn laid her head on the block, Henry VIII was courting Lady Jane, the girl who had been lady-in-waiting, first to Catherine of Aragon, and then to Queen Anne. She married Henry a few days after Anne's execution in 1536, only to die a year later, giving birth to the child who was to become Edward VI. In a gown of white and carrying a lighted taper, the ghost of the twenty-eight-year-old Jane has been seen to emerge from the Queen's old apartments at Hampton Court, wander through the Silverstick Gallery and linger on the Queen's staircase. Her ghost also haunts her old home at Marwell Hall in Hampshire, where she is said to have been married secretly to Henry and spent the happiest year of her life.

Lieutenant Sharp—Shuckburgh Hall, Warwickshire

The effigy of a weeping woman on the Stewkley tomb, in the church at Upper Shuckburgh, is not the only evidence of the tragedy which struck the Shuckburgh family in the early 1800s. Two ghosts linger as a reminder of the day Lieutenant Sharp, of the Bedfordshire militia, went up to the Hall to tell Sir Stewkley he wanted to marry his daughter, an idea the squire didn't like. He forbade his daughter ever to see her soldier boy-friend again, which caused the demented lieutenant to shoot her, and then to blow out his own brains.

Jack Sheppard—Amen Court, London

Sheppard was born in a Spitalfield slum in 1702 and, by the age of twenty-two, had become a legend in his own lifetime as the best known cat burglar in Georgian London. In April 1724 he was caught and the following November hanged at Tyburn, though not before he had done the impossible—escaped from the notorious Newgate prison. It is his daring escape that Sheppard's ghost has been seen re-enacting, clambering along the old prison wall at the end of Dead Man's Walk and dropping to short-lived freedom in Amen Court.

Black Shuck—The Phantom hound

This originated with the Vikings, from the legend of the hound of Odin, dog of war, which the Saxons called Scucca (Shuck) the Devil.

It is called by various names up and down the country; a large black spectral hound, seen at night loping along the lonely lanes of Norfolk, baying as it runs, is called Black Shuck. It has been seen on the coast near Cromer, at Neatishead near the Broads, and at Wicken Fen near Newmarket. In Suffolk they have another name for it—the Galley Trot—a huge hound with glowing eyes which haunts the heathland between Walberswick and Dunwich.

In Lancashire it is Shriker or Hooter, in Yorkshire Padfoot or Guytrash, in Lakeland Boggle or Dobby. The West Country has a name for it, so too have the Fenlands and the Midlands, names such as Hellbeast, Barguest, Shug Monkey, Old Snarlyow, and Gabriels Rache-hounds.

Sarah Siddons—Baker Street, London

Mrs Siddons, one of the most talented beauties of Regency London, was born Sarah Kemble in a Brecon pub called The

Shoulder of Mutton. At eighteen, she married actor William Siddons and went on to become the finest tragedian of the British stage. The site of her former London home in Baker Street, now a London Transport power station, is where her ghost makes its spectral excursions into the twentieth century. Her phantom figure walks through substantial reinforced concrete walls, on the top floor, which is where the actress had her principal bedroom. Mrs Siddons' ghost has also been reported from Bristol where the Theatre Royal, oldest playhouse in England, was the scene of some of her greatest triumphs.

Silky—Black Heddon, Northumberland

Silky was a witch who always wore a black, shiny dress and lived in a shack on the river bank, just below Black Heddon Bridge, where she did some extraordinary things to horses and their riders, causing them to shy or bolt, or stand stock still no matter how much they were urged on. With her death, two centuries ago, the strange happenings have been carried on by her ghost, seen on various occasions by the bridge, known locally as Silky's Bridge and, in recent years, the scene of numerous car accidents.

The Skater—Hickling Broad, Norfolk

Since early in the nineteenth century, the phantom skater of Hickling Broad has been seen from time to time, skimming over the water, as if skating at speed across a frozen surface. This is a spectral flash-back to a tragedy which overtook a young soldier courting a girl who lived on the distant bank of the Broad. To see her more often he took advantage of deep-freeze weather to skate the mile-wide sheet of ice, but failed to heed the warmer days of winter's end, bringing with it treacherous soft patches, one of which gave way under him.

Roger Skelton (The Cauld Lad)—Hylton Castle, near Sunderland, Tyne and Wear

Roger Skelton, a stable lad at Hylton in 1609, is supposedly the ghost which haunted the castle until the 1950s, and is accepted by many as the Cauld Lad of Hylton. Others believe the Claud Lad to be a gremlin-type character out of ancient folklore, a legend revived in the seventeenth century and confused with Skelton's horrible death at the hands of his master, Sir Robert Hylton. Inquest papers relate that the Baron, angered at finding the lad asleep instead of working, seized a pitch fork and stabbed him to death. In a panic he dumped the body in a pond, where it was discovered in 1703. It has all the traumatic ingredients for a sinister haunting separate from the spritely capers of the Cauld Lad.

The Smuggler—Happisburgh, Norfolk

There are very many ghosts of smugglers, but few which appear as horrific as this one. It is a legless body, which comes from the sea, gliding along the road into the village of Happisburgh. Though it appears to be headless, the head is actually hanging by a sinew down its back. In 1765, when this grotesque figure was first seen, it was noted it always disappeared at Well Corner, so the well was searched. From it was taken the decomposing body of a nearly decapitated bearded seafaring man and, separately, in a sack, his legs. At that time Happisburgh was a hotbed of smugglers, and this ghost seems to be an aftermath of a violent quarrel which ended in a brutal killing.

Dorothy Southworth—Samlesbury Old Hall, Lancashire

Locally she is known as the White Lady, first seen in the sixteenth century. But there is uncertainty as to which Dorothy Southworth this White Lady is the ghost of. Legend says she was the tragic daughter of Sir John Southworth, a staunch Catholic, who was shocked when his daughter planned to elope with her Protestant lover, and was secretly thankful his son stopped it by killing the boy and throwing the body into the moat. All this happened in front of his sister who never recovered from the horrific sight and died raving mad. Though, in 1826, human bones were excavated near the river, there are no records of Sir John having a daughter named Dorothy. However, there are records of a lady with the same name, who lived at the same time, three miles away at Pleasington Old Hall. She was Dorothy Winckley, whose first marriage was to a Southworth. Seemingly the legend-makers fictionalised the facts down the centuries.

Lady Stradling—St Donat's Castle, Glamorgan

Lady Stradling's ghost is described as beautiful in high-heeled shoes and a long-trained gown of finest silk. She is one of the family who came to a violent end, murdered by another member of the family who were originally the le Esterlings of Norman descent. According to tradition, her ladyship walks at St Donat's whenever there is the likelihood of misfortune overtaking the House of Stradling.

Lord Strafford—Wheatsheaf Inn, Daventry, Northamptonshire

Strafford, formerly Sir Thomas Wentworth, has made only a single ghostly appearance at this inn and that in the bedroom occupied by Charles I on the eve of the fateful battle of Naseby. Strafford's ghost, although outraged at the King consenting to his lordship's execution, despite the Royal promise that not a hair of his head would be harmed, manifested itself to return good for evil. It warned Charles that to fight Cromwell at Naseby would mean defeat. Many times afterwards the fleeing King was heard to regret not heeding Strafford's ghostly advice.

Lady Ann Streatfield—Chiddingstone, Kent

No spectre of the night this, but visible in broad daylight, a woman on horseback, riding side-saddle, wearing a long skirt and billowing cloak, cantering along the leafy lanes that lead to Chiddingstone Castle. In the eighteenth century, she was the lady of the manor—Ann Streatfield, daughter of the Earl of Leicester of neighbouring Penshurst, who married Henry Streatfield, the family that owned Chiddingstone for 400 years. Her passion was horses; she rode everywhere and her ghost still does today.

Mary Stuart, Queen of Scots—The Talbot, Oundle, Northamptonshire

Mary's ghost haunts in many places, and understandably so, since she suffered many captive years in a string of English castles before being 'untopped' at Fotheringhay. There she left her ghost, though not for long. When the castle was destroyed on the order of King James I, much of the interior decoration, and the oak staircase which Mary used to reach her lofty prison, was bought by William Whitwell, landlord of the Tarbet Inn, at Oundle. Not until some years after, when it was installed at the inn—now called The Talbot—did he know that, with the staircase, he had acquired Mary's ghost.

On her way to imprisonment in Fotheringhay Castle, the martyred Queen stopped at Wansford, lodging at The Haycock, where her ghost is seen in certain of the rooms and corridors, much as it is at The Talbot, to this day.

There is a ghost in the likeness of Mary—tall, slim, in a long dark dress with upright collar—at Southwick House, three miles from Fotheringhay Castle. The two were thought to be connected by a tunnel used by the queen to attend mass undetected, in Southwick's tiny chapel.

A guest staying at Nappa Hall, Wensleydale, in 1878, saw 'a very lovely' ghost wearing a gown of black velvet, and noted that 'her face, figure and general appearance' reminded him of portraits of Mary Stuart, who visited the hall while she was under house arrest at Bolton Castle.

At Beaulieu, Hampshire, ghostly footsteps are heard at night running down the stairs in Palace House, made it is said, by Mary Stuart as she re-enacts the escape she made by using this particular staircase.

Archbishop Simon Sudbury—Canterbury, Kent

Simon Sudbury was murdered in 1381. He was the victim of mob violence, instigated by the Kentish men, led by Wat Tyler. He haunts Canterbury's Sudbury Tower, which he had built to strengthen the bastions of the city. For some years the tower was used as a workshop by a cobbler, who made a note of the movements of the Archbishop's ghost. He described him as tall with a square-cut grey beard and fresh complexion. Which is interesting in itself, since the archbishop was executed. His body lies at Canterbury, while his head is buried at Sudbury, Suffolk.

Sukie—The George and Dragon, West Wycombe, Buckinghamshire

Sukie, a flirtatious sixteen year old who worked as a serving-maid at this High Street coaching inn, in the mid-eighteenth century, became a ghost as a result of a joke that miscarried. She spurned the attentions of the local lads in preference for a ruggedly handsome, prosperous-looking stranger who called frequently. To teach her a lesson the local hopefuls sent her a message to meet her lover in nearby Hell Fire Caves at night, dressed in a bridal gown. Too late did she realise it was all a cruel hoax, as the three most ardent of her admirers sprang at her out of the darkness, jeering and grabbing at her white gown. In the ensuing struggle, Sukie slipped, staggered backwards and struck her skull on the side of the cave as she fell to the ground. The next morning she was dead.

Imogen Swinhoe—Cheltenham, Gloucestershire

This ghost gets a mention in the *Encyclopaedia Britannica* and has been described as 'the most famous case of haunting since the Society for Psychical Research was formed'. At least ten people have seen the figure of a woman of medium height, dressed in Victorian widow's weeds, her face part hidden behind a handkerchief held in the right hand, her fairish hair done up in a bun. It is generally assumed to be the figure of Imogen Swinhoe, second wife of Henry Swinhoe, who lived at Cheltenham, in a house later occupied, in the 1880s by Captain F. W. Despard, whose daughter, Dr Rosina Despard, first saw the ghost. She wrote the first detailed report on it in 1892.

Sir George Sydenham—Sydenham Coombe, Somerset

Sir George's cavalier ghost rides a headless grey horse through Sydenham Coombe, a penance say villagers for being so beastly to Sir Francis Drake. Although Elizabeth Sydenham, his daughter, eventually became Drake's second wife, Sir George disapproved, because Drake was 'so long away at sea'. In fact, he tried to marry her off to someone else, but a meteorite fell in Stogumber churchyard as the bride arrived. She and the guests fled in panic. Sir George blamed Drake, saying he fired a cannon-ball at the church to stop the wedding, although at the time Drake was hundreds of miles away.

Colonel Thomas Sydney—Ranworth Broad, Norfolk

Colonel the Honourable Thomas Sydney, who resided at Ranworth until Christmas 1770, was a hard-drinking, roistering, hunting man. On 31 December of that year, at the biggest meet of the season, he challenged a neighbour to a race, which he won by shooting the other horse, causing its rider to break his neck. At dinner that night, it is reputed, a tall, thin stranger in a black robe appeared and dragged the Colonel out into the darkness, flung him into the saddle of a large black horse and galloped with him towards the Broad, where hissing steam rose from the water as the horse's hooves skimmed the surface. According to legend, every year on 31 December, that scene is repeated as 'the stranger' takes his own.

Sylvia of Llindir—Henllan, Denbighshire

Possibly the best known ghost in Wales haunts the 700 years old Llindir Inn on the edge of the Denbigh Moors. Scores of visitors have reported various ghostly experiences, from seeing the 'Lady of Llindir', to having the clothes dragged from the bed when sleeping in the tiny haunted room under the thatched-covered rafters. Most of the villagers of Henllan believe the rambling building, built in 1229, is haunted by the wraith of Sylvia, the blonde and unfaithful wife of a seaman who strangled her on returning home to find her in the embrace of her lover.

T

Reverend Nathaniel Templeman—Dorchester, Dorset

This reverend gentleman was once Rector of St Peter's, Dorchester, where his ghost appears only in protest against people being sinful in 'his church'. Consequently, he has not been seen very often, though there was one memorable occasion when he was seen by two weary church workers as they rested in the vestry, refreshing themselves with communion wine. As the stern-faced Rector they had both known so well appeared, shaking his head disapprovingly, one man fainted, as the other tried frantically to say the Lord's Prayer.

William Terriss—Adelphi Theatre, London

His real name was William Lewin, but he took the name Terriss and became the idol of the Victorian stage, though not before trying horse-breeding, sheep-farming, gold-mining and life at sea. He died a violent death in December 1897, stabbed as he arrived at the Adelphi stagedoor, victim of a jealous fellow actor, named Richard Prince. While Prince vegetated in Broadmoor, the ghost of Terriss returned to the scene of his stage triumphs. In recent years, it has haunted not only the theatre, but also in the vicinity, including Covent Garden underground station.

Thomas, 4th Duke of Norfolk—Charterhouse, London

The headless ghost that treads the main stairs of the Great Hall of Charterhouse is thought to be the 4th Duke, who fell out with Queen Elizabeth over his proposal to marry Mary Stuart, and lost his head for speaking treason. In the happier years prior to his sudden departure, he made extensive additions to the place, originally built in 1371 as a Carthusian monastery, which possibly accounts for reports of a spectral monk seen in the courts of Washhouse and Masters.

Sarah Thorne—Margate, Kent

Several people claim to have seen the apparition of the Victorian actress, Sarah Thorne, in Margate's old Theatre Royal, where she succeeded her father as manager in 1874. Because the evidence of identification is sparse, there are some who think a more likely explanation for the semi-transparent globular figure, seen moving across the stage, is to be found in the theatre's very early days when an out-of-work actor ended his life by throwing himself from a box.

Sir John Thynne—Longleat, Wiltshire

Sir John Thynne who built Longleat in 1580, is one of its many ghosts. He is thought to be the elderly gentleman, tall and scholarly, who stands by the fireplace in the Red Library and vanishes through the book shelves. A German reporter who, when visiting Longleat, spent a night in the Red Library, claimed Sir John not only appeared but remained several minutes before fading away.

Juliet Tousley—The Ferry Boat Inn, Holywell, Huntingdonshire

Juliet was a delicate and lovely nineteen-year-old when she committed suicide back in 1050. She was so much in love with a local woodcutter, named Tom Zoul, who treated her with such indifference that she could not endure her unhappiness and hanged herself from a willow tree beside the Ouse at Holywell. The place where she was buried, a few yards from the river, was marked with a slab of plain stone, which now forms part of the floor of the Ferry Boat Inn, where her ghost materialises, usually on the night of 17 March, the day Juliet took her own life.

Sir John Towneley—Towneley Hall, Burnley, Lancashire

Sir John was a sixteenth-century landowner whose way with the peasants was to evict them, destroy their homes and take their land. His ruthlessness knew no bounds, even to the extent of evicting an old woman who had just buried her husband. Only when she, too, died of shock did Sir John have pangs of regret. As the months went by he was overcome with remorse and, in his last years, went about muttering his tormented thoughts, just as his ghost does today.

Lady Dorothy Townshend—Raynham Hall, Norfolk

There is no doubt Raynham Hall is haunted since the ghost of 'The Brown Lady' was photographed coming down the great staircase on the afternoon of 19 September 1936. The picture is in the photographic archives of *Country Life* magazine. This sad ghost is that of Dorothy Walpole, sister of the famous Prime Minister, Sir Robert Walpole, and wife of the 2nd Viscount Townshend. She did not, however, die by falling down stairs, or of a broken heart, as legend says. She died in 1726, of smallpox, aged forty. Her ghost has not only been photographed; it has been shot at, by Captain Marryat of *Midshipman Easy* fame. As he fired, 'The Brown Lady' vanished instantly, and the bullet was embedded in a door. Lady Dorothy also haunts nearby Haughton Hall, which her brother built.

Her sudden ghostly appearance in the State Bedroom once frightened the Prince Regent out of his wits.

Sir William de Tracy—Woolacombe, Devon

Sir William, one of the four knights who slaughtered Thomas à Becket on the afternoon of 29 December 1170, has been doing penance for the crime ever since his death. He is cursed to wander at night on Wollacombe Sands, weaving a rope of sand. Some say he haunts Braunton Burrows, where Jack White-Hat's ghost is seen, calling for a boat to ferry him across to Appledore. Whenever the figure hailed a boatman, the summons would be ignored, since it was widely believed that to pick up the man in the great white hat was courting disaster.

Richard Treadwell—Hartley, Kent

Richard Treadwell was an eighteenth-century landlord of Fairby House, at Hartley, whose ghost, at times, is seen in the saddle of his favourite iron-grey mare, making his rounds of Fairby Farm. He haunts but a mile or two from Pennis Lane, where the spectre of a nun has been seen. She was a victim of Thomas Cromwell's lustful soldiers, one of whom hacked off her head rather than let her escape. For years her skull, unearthed by a ploughman, was kept in the study of Pennis Farm.

Mary Anne Treble—Abbots Langley, Hertfordshire

Mary Anne, housekeeper at the vicarage of Abbots Langley, a few years after World War I, died after being given 'a good shaking' because she would not get out of bed one morning after complaining of feeling unwell. On All Saints' Day, Mary's ghost is reputed to walk from the bedroom to her grave, an annual event which crowds from a wide area come to see. The daughter of a former vicar claimed she woke one morning to see the ghostly figure gazing from her bedroom window, while, at the same time, from the cottages opposite, villagers could see Mary's face looking out at them across the churchyard.

Lady Trenchard—Wolfeton House, Dorset

This Lady Trenchard was wife of one of the seventeenth-century lords of the manor, whose restless spirit has walked Wolfeton since she killed herself by cutting her own throat. Less gory is the ghost of the reckless Trenchard who won a wager by driving a coach and horses up the grand staircase, before the cheering household. Since his death, his ghost, at the reins of a spectral coach and pair, has done it many times again. A third ghost is not a Trenchard, but a priest who haunts the gatehouse in which he was imprisoned.

Nan Tuck—Buxted, Sussex

Nan of Buxted haunts the village that branded her a witch,

hounded her to the church where she was refused sanctuary, and then half-drowned her in a stinking duck pond. She escaped her tormentors to flee to the wood which now bears her name, where, said the seventeenth-century villagers, she hanged herself. But did she, or was she lynched? After all her body was buried in consecrated ground, and not at the cross-roads. Perhaps that is also why the wraith of this simple, sensitive girl haunts so purposefully, rushing towards the church along Nan Tuck's lane.

Mary Tudor—Sawston Hall, Cambridgeshire

Bloody Mary, who, in fact, was no more bloody than her father or her sister, Elizabeth, haunts Sawston out of sheer gratitude to the Huddleston family. They saved her life in 1553 by smuggling her out of the back door as a milkmaid, as Northumberland's men stormed the house, intent on taking her prisoner. Not only is the smiling ghost of Mary Tudor reputedly seen in the Tapestry Room, she is *heard* at times, playing the virginal, as she often did for her father, Henry VIII, when visiting Sawston. Another of Sawston's ghosts has lately manifested itself—a night watchman on his rounds in the early hours.

Dick Turpin—Hampstead Heath and elsewhere

Thanks to his fleet-footed Black Bess, highwayman Dick Turpin covered a lot of ground before going to the gallows in 1739. Consequently, his ghost is known to haunt at least half a dozen places. In the saddle of a phantom mare, he has been seen a score of times on Hampstead Heath, presumably heading for the cellars of The Spaniards Inn. At Loughton, in Essex, he rides over Trapps Hill while at Aspley Guise, in Bedfordshire, he has been seen riding down Weathercock Lane towards the old manor. He lurks in the vicinity of the Buckingham village of Woughton-on-the-Green, and, between Hinkley and Nuneaton, is seen or heard cantering along Old Watling Street. It is thought that the ghost of 'a gentleman in green velvet' at the Chequers in Bickley, Kent, may be Turpin, since the highwayman frequented the inn, using a backstairs escape-route to a bedroom where he hid himself in the curtains round an enormous four-poster bed.

William Tylsworth—Old Amersham, Buckinghamshire

William Tylsworth was burned at the stake, one of the martyrs of Amersham condemned for their faith. They are remembered by a memorial in a field just off the Chesham Road, and by the haunting of a pub in Old Amersham. They spent their last night in The Chequers and that is thought to account for the weird shrieking screams echoing through the inn at night. A hooded figure seen in one of the bedrooms could be the ghost of William Tylsworth, or possibly the tormented spirit of his only daughter, forced to light the faggots which burned her father.

U

Johnny Upfold—Peaslake, Surrey

Johnny Upfold was a most pleasant ghost, a funny little figure in tight-fitting trousers and a blue jacket. He was a frequent spectral visitor at a much-ghosted house in Peaslake, near Cranleigh, where he used to sit for hours in the kitchen and not worry anybody. At least half a dozen other phenomena have been experienced in this one-time Royal hunting lodge, some with great regularity, such as 'The Pikeman', the only unpleasant ghost. He occupied a bedroom which adjoined the priest's hiding hole. His presence was only ever felt, although sometimes most forcibly, notably by a small unit of soldiers who occupied part of the house during World War II.

V

Sir Thomas Vaughan—Kington, Herefordshire

The lanes around Kington are ghosted by Sir Thomas and his faithful black bloodhound, sometimes haunting together, sometimes separately, but never very far from Hergest Court, which was, for years, the seat of the Vaughan family. Sir Thomas, known as Black Vaughan, was beheaded in 1483, since when there have been isolated reports of a strange haunting at Hergest Court—Sir Thomas' head seen hovering over the still water of the moat.

Sir Edmund Verney—Middle Claydon, Buckinghamshire

Sir Edmund, standard bearer to King Charles at the battle of Edgehill, refused to surrender the colours when overrun by Cromwell's army. 'My life is my own. My Standard is my King's', he shouted. Though the Roundheads killed him, they were unable to prise the standard from his grasp, so cut off his hand. Later the standard was recaptured with the hand still clasped to it. It was taken back for burial at Claydon House, the Verney home since 1471. There the ghost of Sir Edmund, without a right hand, has been seen searching for his missing limb. While he tends to concentrate on the vicinity of the Red Stairs, there is a Grey Lady seen at times in the Rose Room. It is thought that she may be the ghost of Florence Nightingale, a frequent guest at Claydon after her sister, Parthenope, married Sir Harry Verney in 1857. Another haunt of the famous nurse was the Military Chapel in the grounds of Netley Abbey, in Hampshire.

The Viking—Canvey Island, Essex

This ghost is 6ft tall, fierce-looking, with long moustaches and a beard. He wears a horned-helmet and a belted jerkin of coarse leather, similar to the ribbons of leather wound round his legs. Fishermen and wild-fowlers who have seen him, say he strides out of the sea, across the mudflats at Canvey Point, a long sword swinging at his belt. All are agreed that this is the ghost of a Viking warrior, possibly one of the invasion army led by Halvdan in 894, and routed by King Alfred's son, Edward the Elder.

Barbara Villiers—Duchess of Cleveland, Chiswick Mall, London

Wife of the Earl of Castlemaine and later Duchess of Cleveland, Barbara Villiers was always first favourite of Charles II's mistresses. For ten years, from May 1660, she had great attraction for the King, largely because her knowledge of 'all the tricks of Aretin'. In her old age, she became a Roman Catholic, retired to Walpole House, Chiswick, and died there of dropsy, aged sixty-nine. To the end, she prayed hard for the restoration of her lost beauty. According to some, her ghost is still doing so, pacing to and fro and pleading with begging hands in front of the drawing room windows.

George Villiers, 2nd Duke of Buckingham—Skeldergate, York

Despite being a favourite of King Charles II, the Duke died a pauper. He also died in disgrace, having upset the Court by fighting a duel over the Countess of Shrewsbury, his mistress. The Countess watched, dressed as a pageboy, while Buckingham skewered her husband. He spent his last years in York where he had a town house in Skeldergate, close to where the Cock and Bottle Inn is today and where his ghost is now active. Not very far away was the gazebo where he is said to have tried desperately to make gold from base metals, in a last attempt to clear himself of bankruptcy. On his death bed at Kirkby Moorside, the Duke asked to be taken back to die in York, but he was considered too ill. So his spectral self returned when his body was taken to Westminster to be buried in an unmarked grave.

SS 'Violet'—Goodwin Sands, off Kent

The Channel packet *Violet*, bound for Dover from Ostende on an ink-black February night in the 1850s, hit the dreaded Goodwin Sands and was lost with all hands. The crew of the North

Sands lightship saw it happen, powerless to help. Ninety years on, shortly after the start of World War II, seven crewmen on the South Goodwin lightship watched, horrified and helpless, as it all happened again; an old-style paddle steamer with tall, raked funnel, lights blazing, headed out of a swirling blizzard, full speed for the devouring sands. They had seen the phantom packet-boat *Violet* reliving her last moments before disaster struck nearly a century before.

W

John Walford—Stowey, Somerset

Dark, handsome and twenty-four was John Walford, a Somerset charcoal burner who, in the June of 1789, had to wed a local girl named Jenny because she'd had his baby. He always boasted his love for another village beauty, Ann Rice, and his overwhelming desire for her caused him to lose his self-control and kill his bride of only seventeen days. All his good looks and popularity could not save him from hanging, or from haunting, at a place still known as Walford's Gibbet, just as the place where Jenny's ghost haunts is named Dead Woman's Ditch after the murder spot.

St John Wall—Chingle Hall, Goosnaugh, Lancashire

The phantom monk in Franciscan habit, frequently seen at Chingle, is thought to be the martyred St John, who was hanged, drawn and quartered in 1679, for preaching Roman Catholicism. He was born at the Hall and there are many who believe his skull is buried somewhere here. A door which opens and closes unaided is a daily and nightly occurrence at Chingle; rappings and tappings are commonplace; so too is the sight of the ghostly figure crossing the stone bridge over the moat, entering the porch and moving up the stairs, finally and suddenly vanishing in the little bedroom over the entrance porch.

Mary Ward—Morton upon Swale, North Yorkshire

Mary, an eighteenth-century servant girl, employed in a house at Romanby, near Northallerton, was murdered after finding out that her allegedly reputable employer was the brains behind a gang of forgers. She passed on her discovery in gossip, which eventually reached the ear of her master, who arranged for her to be called away urgently to visit her sick mother. During her journey she disappeared in the vicinity of Moreton Bridge, the place where her restless wraith has since been seen by many.

Lady Blanche de Warrene—Rochester, Kent

Lady Blanche died at the top of the Round Tower of Rochester Castle, killed by an arrow from the bow of Sir Ralph de Capo, the man she loved. Looking up from beyond the moat and seeing her struggling with Sir Gilbert de Clare, the knight she had rejected for him, Sir Ralph took a bow and let fly a carefully aimed arrow which hit de Clare. But his armour deflected it into the bosom of Lady Blanche, who died at his feet. That same night her ghost walked the battlements as it has done many times since, a white-robed figure, with an arrow in her chest.

Sarah Whitehead—Bank of England, London

This ghost has long been dubbed the Black Nun of the Bank of England, though, in fact, Sarah Whitehead never was a nun, but the sister of Philip Whitehead, a trainee cashier hanged in 1811 for forgery. When news of her brother's tragic end was accidentally broken to Sarah, the shock sent her mad. Dressed in mourning, her face heavily veiled, she went daily to the bank to inquire after her brother, then to pace up and down outside, waiting for him. Even when she died twenty-five years on, she didn't cease her vigil; her ghost goes on waiting, haunting in the bank's trim little garden, formerly St Christopher's churchyard, in which Sarah was buried.

John Whitfield—Barrock Hill, Cumbria

This notorious highwayman plagued the roads and tracks around

Carlisle in the eighteenth century, until a sharp-eyed boy who saw Whitfield attack and shoot a traveller, brought him to justice by finding a button from the ruffian's coat at the scene of the crime. Whitfield paid with his life, gibbeted alive on Barrock Hill in 1777. After a week of agony, he was mercifully shot by a passing coach driver and, for 200 years following his death, travellers on the old road to Carlisle have reported hearing the ghostly screams and moans of the dying man.

The Sergeant's Wife—Birdcage Walk, London

'I do solemnly declare that when on guard ... about half past one in the morning, I perceived the figure of a woman, without a head, rise from the earth at a distance of about two feet before me.' Those are the sworn words of Coldstream Guardsman George Jones, stationed at Wellington Barracks in 1804, one of several sentries who saw this ghost, dressed in a red-striped gown, near Cockpit Steps, St James' Park. An Army inquiry produced evidence of a long-forgotten murder of some twenty years before, when a sergeant in the Coldstreams killed his wife and threw her body into St James' Park lake, after cutting off her head.

Willy Willcock—Polperro, Cornwall

Jonathan Couch in his *History of Polperro*, written in 1856, mentions the ghost of Willy Willcock. He reputedly haunts a cave below Chapel Hill, entered from behind the quay and stretching westwards to under the next village of Landavedy. Since about the 1780s, when Willcock squeezed through a narrow gap at the rear of the cave and died in the bowels of the hill, it's been called Willy Willcock's Hole. The noises coming from the cave, plainly heard in the quiet of the night, are said to be the shrieks of the dying man.

Fly-boy Willie—Lindholme, South Yorkshire

Willie is one of our aircrew chaps who didn't quite make it back to base during World War II. He's 'an extraordinary ghost' says his one-time commanding officer, and a familiar figure around the

RAF station at Lindholme, from where the Wellington bomber, in which he crashed, took off for a raid on Germany in 1944. Willie died with the rest of the crew when the shot-up aircraft, limping home, plummeted into a bog between the Humber and Doncaster. The ex-commanding officer well remembers both Willie and his ghost: 'We often used to hear him come in, clump up the stairs in his big flying boots and clump back down again. My son . . . saw and spoke to him once. He was in full flying kit and passed the time of day.'

The Willington Wraith—near Newcastle, Tyne and Wear

Certainly this is one of the most publicised of the north east's supernatural happenings of the mid-nineteenth century. For twelve years, a family lived with a poltergeist at Willington Mill on Tyneside. In addition, at least five apparitions were seen. Before the turn of the century, the place was demolished and the poltergeist with it. But, of the various ghosts, two survived to carry on haunting the busy road from Newcastle to North Shields. The spectral figures sometimes seen are a woman with eyeless sockets, and a tall, bearded priest. Locally it is said the woman committed suicide, after the priest had refused to hear her confession to a murder on the old mill site.

John Winter—North Road station, Darlington, Durham

North Road was the first ever railway station in the world, built in the 1840s for passengers on the original Darlington to Stockton line. It is now a railway museum with a ghost as its most macabre exhibit. He was first encountered on a December night in 1890, the shadowy figure of a station clerk in Victorian railway uniform, coming out of a coalhouse with a black retriever at his heels. He was identified as a man named Winter who had committed suicide on the station. The night-watchman who saw the ghost, took a swing at it and cut his knuckles on the wall behind.

Dr James Wood—St John's, Cambridge

On his death, in 1839, Dr Wood was Master of St John's. He had come a long way from the days when, as an undergraduate, he was so short of money that he packed his clothes with straw for extra warmth, and studied sitting on the stairs leading to his rooms, because that was the only place where there was a candle he could read by. It is the hard-up student James Wood who haunts St John's, his ghostly figure huddled on the staircase in the Second Court of the college.

The Novice of Woodchester Park—near Stroud, Gloucestershire

For more than a century, the half-finished mansion at Woodchester has looked like every Hollywood producer's dream of a haunted house, in a setting which even Hitchcock at his best would have difficulty in matching. Two miles of wooded parkland, with a thin vapour-like mist rising from the chain of lakes on a bright moonlight night, is something which puts the imagination on overtime. But the ghosts of Woodchester Park are far from imagined, though of the sixteen apparitions sighted over the years, not all have been given positive identities.

Apart from a coach and four seen phantomising between the rear gates of the park and the deserted mansion, the most interesting of this host of ghosts is the Novice of Woodchester. This young Dominican monk from the nearby priory left behind a ghost the day he drowned, while skating on one of the frozen lakes in the picturesque valley, early this century. Among the other supernatural park dwellers are:

a headless horseman who rides round a small island in the fifth lake;

a seventeenth-century nobleman, also on horseback, riding along the drive;

a Roman centurion passing up and down near the gates on the south road;

the spectre of Thomas Arundel, who owned the park at the time of the Reformation and who died for his Catholic beliefs.

In the eighteenth century the Ducie family built a mansion in the park, of which only the gates and a summer house remain. The present mansion was begun by William Leigh, a nineteenth-century convert to Catholicism, who built the priory in 1846, but ran out of money before the house could be completed, since when it has been inhabited only by bats.

Arnold Woodruffe—Theatre Royal, London

Best known of all London's many ghosts is that of Drury Lane's Theatre Royal—the Man in Grey—believed to be a dandy of the late eighteenth century, young, slim, handsome, stabbed to death in a stage brawl. He has been seen by no fewer than sixty people at various times, always during matinees, never at night. A spiritualist who went into a trance in the theatre, claimed afterwards the ghost was that of Arnold Woodruffe, and dubbed it 'Friend Arnold' because to see the Man in Grey at Drury Lane is a good luck omen for whatever show is running at the theatre.

Alderman Edward Wooler—Yorkshire Museum, York

The ghost of Alderman Wooler, a Darlington solicitor, was seen in the museum library, in 1953, by the caretaker who encountered the figure looking for a book. Shown a photograph of Edward Wooler, who died in the 1920s, the caretaker instantly recognised the man he'd seen the night before, rummaging among the volumes. The book the ghost took from the shelf and dropped on the floor was *Antiquities and Curiosities of the Church*, presented to the library by the Alderman. Across the road, York's Theatre Royal, is haunted by a novice nun, an echo from the days when St Leonard's Hospice stood on the site.

Sir Christopher Wren—Old Court House, Hampton Court, Middlesex

Wren, builder of fifty-two of the City's churches and St Paul's Cathedral, also rebuilt Wolsey's Hampton Court Palace for William and Mary. It took five years, during which time he lived on the job at the Old Court House where his ghost is said to walk on the anniversary of his death. For a number of years, the sound of inexplicable footsteps climbing the stairs has been heard on the night of 26 February.

Lady Anne Wroughton—Wilcot, Wiltshire

Lady Anne is thought to be the original of the White Lady of Wilcot. In that Wiltshire village, near Pewsey, a tale is told of how Squire Wroughton turned his young wife, Anne, out into the snow on Christmas Eve, falsely accusing her of infidelity. She stumbled as far as she was able before collapsing with cold and exhaustion and there her lifeless body was found next day. From that time on a white figure has sometimes been seen, either gliding along the lane where she died, or on Lady Bridge spanning the Kennet and Avon canal.

Wroughton the Recluse—Easterton, Wiltshire

Wroughton the Recluse lived at Maggot Castle, to the south of Devizes. All that is left of what was once a sizeable eighteenth-century mansion belonging to the Wroughton family, are grass-covered ruins, a ghost and a legend that several of the servant girls employed there mysteriously disappeared. The recluse died on his own door-step, returning home one night in a drunken stupor. He overturned his carriage and broke his neck, leaving Maggot Castle to become a ruin haunted by the sound of horses galloping and a coach being driven furiously up the drive towards the ruins.

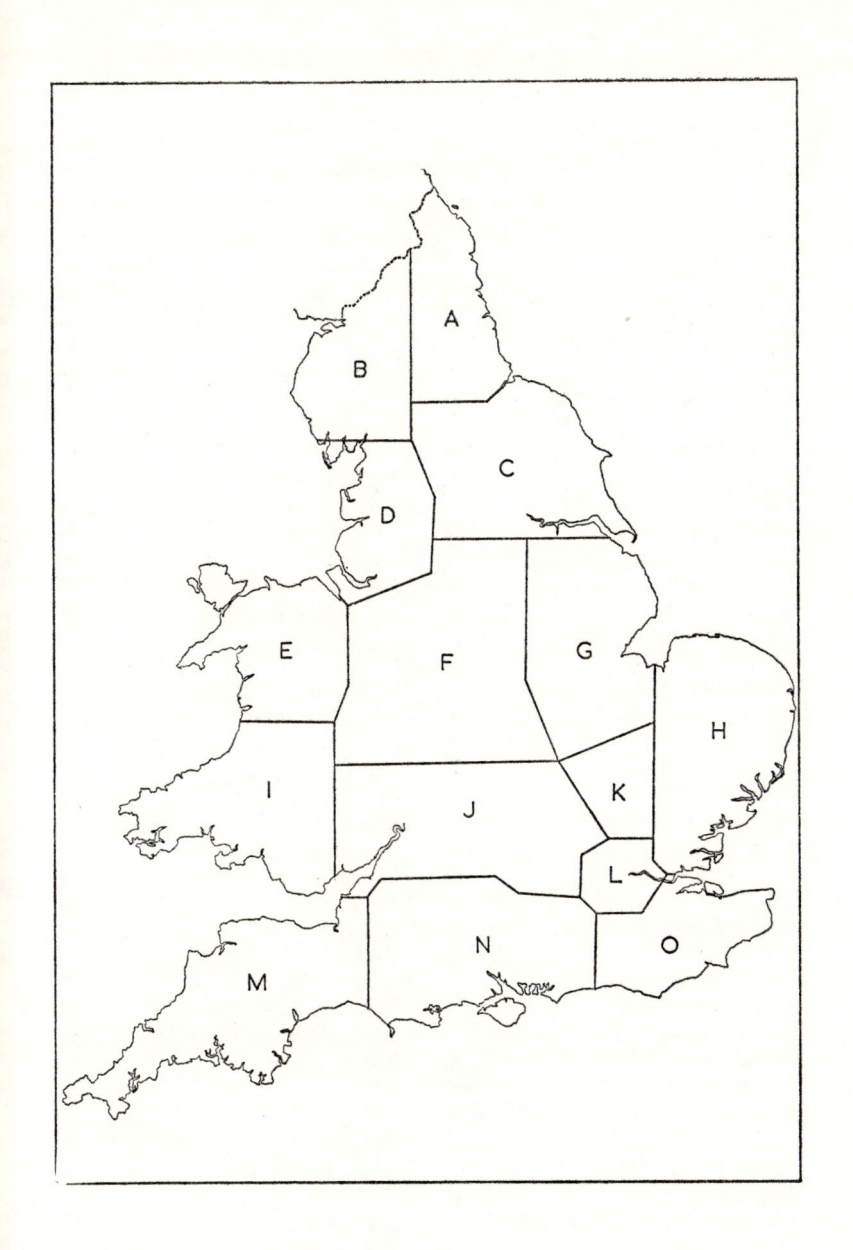

KEY TO MAP

Jeremiah Abershaw	L	Queen Boadicea	G
Lady Abigail	B	Boatswain	F
Elizabeth Adams	J	Queen Anne	L
Father Ambrose	D	Lady Mary Bolles	C
Bishop Lancelot Andrews	L	Lady Boston	L
Queen Anne's Messenger	L	William Boulter	N
Lord John Angerstein	L	John Bradshaw	L
Annie	L	Babes of Bramber	O
Fred Archer	H	John Breed	O
Anne Armstrong	A	The Bridesmaids of Gt Melton	H
Archie Armstrong	A	Sir Barney Brograve	H
Squire John Arscott	M	Emily Brontë	C
King Athelstan	A	Rupert Chawner Brooke	K
Jack Arthur	A	Edward Broome	F
King Arthur	N	Theophilus Broome	N
Lady Blanche Arundell	N	Bella Brown	A
Lady St Aubyn	L	Lilly Browne	L
The Ballet Dancer	L	Marion de la Bruere	F
Old Barbery	A	Lord Buckhurst	L
Mrs Barnes	N	Marmaduke Buckle	C
Elizabeth Barton	L	John Buckstone	L
William Batt	C	Louisa Bunting	H
Ghost of Beachy Head	O	Clara Burnett	J
Lady Beauclark	D	Thomas Busby	C
Thomas à Becket	O	2nd Marquess of Bute	I
Abe Beer	M	Squire Butler	K
'Flasker' Beesley	O	Dr Butts	K
Lydia Bell	C	Admiral John Byng	L
Father Benedictus	L	Elizabeth Bynge	N
Jeremy Bentham	L	Sir Walter Calverley	C
Derek Bentley	L	Lady Frederick Campbell	O
Sir Bertram of Bothal	A	Kitty Canham	H
The Bettiscombe Skull	M	Giles Cannard	N
Lady de Bevere	C	Brother Cantata	O
Alice Birch	J	The Captain	M
The Black Canon	C	Maude Carew	H
The Black Horse	C	Billie Carleton	L
Trumpet Major Blandford	N	Joan Carn	M
Mary Blandy	J	Lady Louisa Carteret	N
Lady de Blenkinsopp	B	Queen Catherine	K

The Cavaliers	C	William Drury	N
Abbot Chard	M	Charlotte Dymond	M
King Charles I	L	Sir Robert Earnley	N
Aunt Charlotte	N	Lady Editha	F
Darkie Chase	M	Edward, the Martyr	N
Miser Chickett	N	Elaine	F
Lizzie Church	L	Queen Elizabeth	L
Pieman Clibbon	K	King Ella	H
Rosamund Clifford	J	The Evangelist	N
Jane Maria Clousen	L	Faith	C
The Long Coastguardsman	H	Guy Fawkes	C
Grizelle Cochrane	A	Lady Katherine Ferrers	J
Leathery Coit	C	Finny	M
Betty Coke	F	Mary Fitton	F
Henry Coker	N	Sir Reginald Fitz Urse	B
Thomas Cole	L	Sarah Fletcher	J
Lady Constantia Coleraine	L	Dorothy Forster	A
Sam Collins	L	Jonas Fosbrooke	K
William Constable	C	Freddie Fredericks	L
Kraster and Dorothy Cook	B	Reverend Maurice Frost	J
Mary Anne Cotton	A	Edwin Fry	J
Bishop Coverdale	L	The Fugitive	M
Crier of Claife	B	Farmer Gammon	M
Kit Crewbucket	F	Jimmy Garlickhythe	L
Tom Crocker	M	Kitty Garthwaite	C
Oliver Cromwell	L	Sir John Gates	H
Squire Cunliffe	D	Piers Gaveston	C
The Cyclist	F	George II	L
Young Lord Dacre	O	George III	L
Grace Darling	A	George IV	O
Rachel Darrell	N	The Ghost Train	N
Will Darrell	N	Sir Walter Giffard	M
David Davies	M	Tobias Gill	H
John Dawson	D	Gilsland Boy	B
Lady Dering	O	Henry Girdlestone	G
Lady Anna Derwentwater	A	Judge John Glanville	M
Doctor Dick	I	Robert Glover	J
Charles Dickens	L	Police Sergeant Goddard	L
Sir Everard Digby	G	Edward Golding	J
Dorothy Dingle	M	Margaret Gould	M
Benjamin Disraeli	J	Charlie Gordon	A
Edward Dobsod	F	Lady Elizabeth Gray	K
Lady Dodington	N	The Grenadier	L
William Doggett	N	Sir Fulke Greville	F
Father Dominique	J	Lady Jane Grey	L
Nurse Dowdall	C	Jo Grimaldi	L
Sir Francis Drake	M	Lady Anne Grimston	K

Hannah Grundy	C	Lady Jane	G
The Guardsman	L	William Jarman	J
Martha Gunn	O	Mary Jay	M
'George' Gutsell	O	Old Jeffrey	G
Rosamund Guy	G	Judge Jeffreys	M
Mistress Eleanor Gwynn	L	Jimmy	L
The Hairy Hands	M	Sir Strange Jocelyn	K
Lady Constance Hall	L	John the Jibber	A
John Hampden	J	Dean Jones	J
King Harold	O	Harry Jones	J
George Hastilow	F	Brother Joseph	M
Sir Henry Hawkins	L	Herbert Kay	L
George Haydock	D	Emily Kaye	O
Maud Heath	N	Bishop Thomas Ken	N
King Henry VI	B	Captain William Kidd RN	L
King Henry VIII	L	Ned King	D
Lulu von Herkomer	L	Bishop Lacy	M
Vincent Herman	L	Marie Lairre	H
Herne, the Hunter	L	Percy Lambert	L
Tom Hewson	C	Ann Lamplugh	B
Reverend Samson Hieron	O	Sir William Langhorne	L
Edward Higgins	F	Archbishop Laud	J
Abbess St Hilda	C	T. E. Lawrence	N
Sir Rowland Hill	F	Lizzie Lawton	M
Squire Hilliard	M	Widow Leaky	M
Anne Hinchfield	L	David Leany	O
Lady Elizabeth Hoby	J	Jane Leeson	J
Tom Hoggett	C	Sir Piers Legh	F
Earl of Holland	K	Dan Leno	L
Ada Holmes	A	Armine L'Estrange	H
Queen Catherine	L	Ladies of Levens	B
Lady Mary Howard	M	Field Marshal Lord Ligonier	N
Dr Michael Hudson	G	Lady Lisgar	F
William Hunter	H	Dame Alice Lisle	N
Lady Ursula Hynde	K	Catherine Tylney Long	L
Brother Ignatius	G	Major Ralph Longworth	D
Prince Imperial of France	N	Lord Lovell	J
Elizabeth Ingilby	C	Sir James Lowther	B
Sir Henry Irving	C	Lucette	D
Mary Isaac	L	Lady Luvibund	O
Rabbi Isaacs	H	Charles Macklin	L
Queen Isabella	H	The Mad Monk	M
Mrs It	J	Baldwin Malet	N
Peg-leg Jack	O	Sir Geoffrey de Mandeville	L
Spring-heel Jack	L	Lord Marney	H
Captain Jacques	N	Mother Marnes	L
James, Duke of Monmouth	M	George Marsh	D

Elsie Marshall	L	The Phantom Fiddler	N
Lady Margaret Massingberd	G	The Phantom Funeral	F
Archdeacon Edmund Mervyn	N	The Phantom General	L
'Spider' Marshall	H	The Phantom Monks of St	
Martha	O	Dunstan's	L
Martyn's Ape	N	The Phantom Nurse	L
Bonnie May Marye	B	The Phantom Persian	L
John (Topsy Turvy) Massey	J	The Phantom Spitfire	L
Mad Maude	J	Old Doctor Phene	L
Lady May	F	Mademoiselle Pinard	O
Old Charlie Miles	N	The Plate-layer	L
Johnnie Minney	K	Lady Plumley	M
'Old Moses'	J	Lady Margaret de Pomeroy	M
Colonel Mulliner	L	Alexander Pope	L
Irene Munro	O	The Prehistoric Man	N
Awd Nance	C	Thomas Pryde	O
Nance	C	Sir Robert Pye	J
The Naseby Phenomenon	F	Radiant Boy	B
Georgiana Naylor	O	Rahere	L
Grace Naylor	O	Sir Walter Raleigh	L
Geoffrey Netherwood	L	George Ransley	O
Reverend Percy Newall	N	The Rapist	N
Polly Nicholls	L	Margaret Reay	L
Thomas Nicholson	B	The Redhead	G
Ivor Novello	L	Sir Henry Rich	L
Richard Oastler	C	Hugh Ripley	C
Kate Oatway	M	Amy Robsart	J
Jack O'Cassiobury	L	Lady Rokeby	A
Peg O'Nell	D	Rosata	K
The Old Maids of Llangollen	G	Donald Ross	L
Dickey O'Tunstead	F	Christopher Round	K
Donna Leonora Oviedo	G	King William Rufus	N
Brother Pacificus	H	Prince Rupert	J
Paddy	D	Ghost of Runway I	L
Madam Papillon	F	Lady Scamler	H
Sir Hubert Parry	N	Dame Dorothy Selby	O
John Paslew	D	Sellis	L
Elizabeth Pateman	K	The Severed Arm	F
Lady Joan Pelham	O	Lady Jane Seymour	L
Kate Penfound	M	Lieutenant Sharp	F
Mrs Sibell Penn	L	Jack Sheppard	L
Captain Henry Penruddock	N	Black Shuck	H
Sir Josceline Percy	C	Sarah Siddons	L
Peter the Great	N	Silky	A
The Phantom of the A23	O	The Skater	H
The Phantom Chicken of		Roger Skelton (The Cauld Lad)	A
Highgate	L	The Smuggler of Happisburgh	H

Dorothy Southworth	D	Johnny Upfold	N
Lady Stradling	G	Sir Thomas Vaughan	J
Lord Strafford	F	Sir Edmund Verney	J
Lady Ann Streatfield	O	The Viking	H
Mary Stuart	G	Barbara Villiers	L
Archbishop Simon Sudbury	O	George Villiers	C
Sukie	J	S S *Violet*	O
Imogen Swinhoe	J	John Walford	M
Sir George Sydenham	M	St John Wall	D
Colonel Thomas Sydney	H	Mary Ward	C
Sylvia of Llindir	G	Lady Blanche de Warrene	O
Rev Nathaniel Templeman	N	Sarah Whitehead	L
William Terriss	L	John Whitfield	B
Thomas, 4th Duke of Norfolk	L	The Sergeant's Wife	L
Sarah Thorne	O	Willy Willcock	M
Sir John Thynne	N	Fly-Boy Willie	G
Juliet Tousley	K	The Willington Wraith	A
Sir John Towneley	D	John Winter	A
Lady Dorothy Townshend	H	Dr James Wood	K
Sir William de Tracy	M	The Novice of Woodchester Park	J
Richard Treadwell	O		
Mary Anne Treble	J	Arnold Woodruffe	L
Lady Trenchard	N	Alderman Edward Wooler	C
Nan Tuck	O	Sir Christopher Wren	L
Mary Tudor	K	Lady Anne Wroughton	N
Dick Turpin	L	Wroughton the Recluse	N
William Tylsworth	J	Sir Robert Wynne	I

BIBLIOGRAPHY

Alexander, Marc. *Haunted Castles* (Muller, 1974)
——. *Haunted Inns* (Muller, 1973)
——. *Phantom Britain* (Muller, 1975)
Archer, Fred. *Ghost Writer* (W. H. Allen, 1966)
Armstrong, Warren. *Sea Phantoms* (Odhams Press, 1963)
Bardens, Dennis. *Ghosts and Hauntings* (Fontana, 1965)
Baring-Gould, Reverend S. *Early Reminiscences 1834–1864* (John Lane, The Bodley Head, 1923)
Bord, Janet and Colin. *Mysterious Britain* (Paladin, 1974)
Braddock, Joseph. *Haunted Houses* (Batsford, 1956)
Branston, Brian. *Beyond Belief* (Weidenfeld and Nicolson, 1974)
——. *The Call of Chambercobe* (Chronicle Press, Ilfracombe, 1964)
Carter, George Goldsmith. *The Goodwin Sands* (Constable, 1953)
Chambers, Michael. *London the Secret City* (Ocean Books, 1974)
Christian, Roy. *Ghosts and Legends* (David and Charles, 1972)
Coxe, Anthony Hippisley. *Haunted Britain* (Hutchinson, 1973)
Coxhead, J. R. W. *Ghosts in Devon* (Town and Country Press, 1972)
Daniel, Clarence. *Ghosts of Derbyshire* (Dalesman, 1973)
Day, J. Wentworth. *In Search of Ghosts* (Muller, 1969)
——. *A Ghost Hunter's Game Book* (Muller, 1958)
——. *Here are Ghosts and Witches* (Batsford, 1954)
——. *Essex Ghosts* (Spurbooks, 1973)
Dixon, Janet. *Welsh Ghosts* (James Pike, 1975)
Eyre, Kathleen. *Lancashire Ghosts* (Dalesman, 1974)
Findler, Gerald. *Ghosts of the Lake Counties* (Dalesman, 1969)
Formon, Joan. *Haunted East Anglia* (Fontana, 1976)
Green, Andrew. *Our Haunted Kingdom* (Wolfe, 1973)
——. *Ghosts of the South East* (David and Charles, 1976)
Green, Celia and McCreery, Charles. *Apparitions* (Hamish Hamilton, 1975)
Haining, Peter. *Ghosts, The Illustrated History* (Sidgwick and Jackson, 1974)
Halifax, Lord. *Lord Halifax's Ghost Book* (Fontana, 1961)
Hallam, Jack. *Haunted Inns of England* (Wolfe, 1972)
——. *Ghosts of London* (Wolfe, 1975)

——. *Ghosts of the North* (David and Charles, 1976)
Harper, G. C. *Haunted Houses* (Chapman and Hall, 1907)
Harris, Henry. *Cornish Saints and Sinners* (John Lane, The Bodley Head, 1906)
Harries, John. *Ghosts Hunters' Road Book* (Muller, 1968)
    The Highways and Byways (series) (Macmillan)
Hole, Christina. *Haunted England* (Batsford, 1940)
Hopkins, R. Thurston. *Adventures with Phantoms* (Quality Press, 1946)
Holzer, Hans. *Ghosts I've Met* (Herbert Jenkins, 1966)
——. *The Great British Ghost Hunt* (W. H. Allen, 1976)
Hunt, Robert. *Cornish Customs and Superstitions* (Tor Mark Press, 1972)
Ingram, John. *The Haunted Homes and Family Legends* (Gibbings, 1897)
    The King's England (series) ed Arthur Mee (Hodder & Stoughton)
Legg, Rodney. *A Guide to Dorset Ghosts* (Dorset Publishing Co, 1969)
Lofthouse, Jessica. *Lancashire's Fair Face* (Robert Hale, 1952)
Ludlam, Harry. *The Restless Ghosts of Ladye Place* (Foulsham, 1967)
Mackenzie, Andrew. *Apparitions and Ghosts* (Barker, 1971)
——. *Frontiers of the Unknown* (Barker, 1968)
Maple, Eric. *The Realm of Ghosts* (Pan, 1967)
Metcalfe, John. *Discovering Ghosts* (Shire, 1972)
Mitchell, Anne. *Ghosts Along the Thames* (Spurbooks, 1972)
Mitchell, John, V. *Ghosts of an Ancient City* (Cerialis Press, 1974)
Mitchell, W. R. *Yorkshire Ghosts* (Dalesman, 1969)
Norman, Diana. *The Stately Ghosts of England* (Muller, 1963)
O'Donnell, Elliott. *Haunted Britain* (Rider, 1948)
——. *Haunted Churches* (Quality Press, 1939)
——. *Byways of Ghostland* (Rider, 1911)
Price, Harry. *The Most Haunted House in England* (Longmans, 1940)
Reynolds, James. *Gallery of Ghosts* (Creative Age, 1949)
    Romantic Britain, ed Tom Stephenson (Odhams Press, 1937)
Sampson, C. *Ghosts of the Broads* (The Yachtsman Publishing Co, 1931)
Sergeant, Philip W. *Historic British Ghosts* (E.P. Publishing, 1974)
Squires, Patricia. *The Ghosts In the Mirror* (Muller, 1972)
Stevens, William Oliver. *Unbidden Guests* (Allen and Unwin, 1949)
Styles Showell. *Welsh Walks and Legends* (John Jones of Cardiff, 1972)
Taylor, Alfred. 'The Odd Spot' (Yorkshire Evening Post, 1965)
Tebbutt, C. F. 'Huntingdon Folklore' (Cambs & Hunts Archaeological Society, 1952)
Tegner, M. A. Henry. *Ghosts of the North Country* (Frank Graham, 1974)
Travis, Peter. *In Search of the Supernatural* (Wolfe, 1975)
Turner, B. *A Place in the Country* (Weidenfeld & Nicholson, 1972)
Turner, James. *Ghosts of the South West* (David and Charles, 1973)

Underwood, Peter. *Gazetteer of British Ghosts* (Souvenir Press, 1971)
——. *Haunted London* (Harrap, 1973)
——. and Tabori, Paul. *The Ghosts of Borley* (David and Charles, 1973)
Weekend Book of Ghosts, ed R. Whittington-Egan (Associated Newspapers Ltd, 1975)
Wiltshire, Kathleen. *Ghosts and Legends of the Wiltshire Countryside* (Compton Russell, 1973)
Wood, G. Bernard. *Secret Britain* (Cassell, 1968)

GHOSTS OF THE NORTH by Jack Hallam
The north of England is agog with ghosts. It is a spine-chilling collection with full 'how-to-get-there' details for iron-nerved ghost-hunters
8½ × 5½in

GHOSTS OF WESSEX by Keith B. Poole
This collection of eery stories from Berkshire, Dorset, Hampshire, Oxford, Somerset, Avon and Wiltshire offers an enticing combination of fact and legend
8½ × 5½in

GHOSTS OF THE SOUTH EAST by Andrew Green
Covering Kent, Sussex and Surrey, the ghostly stories offer interesting insights into family histories and intrigues as well as haunting reading
8½ × 5½in

GHOSTS IN THE SOUTH WEST by James Turner
The ghosts of Devon, Cornwall, Dorset and Somerset range from a *crime passionel* in the wolds of Bodmin Moor to a haunting in Dorchester with interesting sidelights on country life
8½ × 5½in   Illustrated